This well-written, to the devastating takable way. Reco heart that connects and feels for others. This is a roadmap to recognition, a salve for the injured, and a resounding call to action to the church and all who profess to believe. This WE thing can be eradicated. Rebecca Commean has lived through the fire and voluntarily jumped back into the flames to pull out our collective consciousness. I now feel the urgency of action needed!

—**Consuella Meeks**, Meeks Enterprises, LLC

Empowering and unintimidating! Rebecca Commean defines all different forms of abuse with easy-to-picture personal examples. I love how this book educates the reader on both hard stops toward abuse and a path out of abuse. Working with young women as a labor and delivery nurse, I see where a handbook like this, with all the resources listed in the back pages, should be at the fingertips of every female. Thank you, Becky, for recognizing abuse in all forms and providing the education needed to stop it.

—**Elizabeth Culhane**, RN

Domestic abuse is a prevalent horror that exists right under our noses. For those of us who live a life dedicated to Christ, it often exists right under our comfortable religious traditions, Sunday sermons, and worship experiences. Becky's story of abuse and trauma shows that DV is frequently ignored and even justified by the leaders and congregants in our places of worship; it's a testament to the work that needs to be done, in and out of the church, to address domestic violence and its impact on the survivor and the community at large. The church has failed many women who have suffered at the hands of abusers, and Becky's strength as a survivor is evident in the words she writes and her passion for the subject.

—**Sara White**, Founder, Fresh Beginnings Safe House

Passionate and practical, *Is This Domestic Abuse?* is not only for those experiencing abuse but also for their loved ones and faith communities. For the abused seeking answers to the questions, "Is this abuse? Am I in an abusive relationship? What can I possibly do about it?" this book infuses possibility, confidence, and hope for how to break from an unhealthy relationship safely and realistically. For loved ones and leaders in Christian churches, Rebecca Commean offers strong words from personal stories about what to do and not do to love well those experiencing abuse.

Borne of her battles, losses, and victories, Commean shares some hard truths to help and guide the abused woman and the Christian community if we, as readers, have ears to hear and hearts to receive. Faith-based or not, any reader WILL FIND guidance and checklists to start taking steps today to protect themselves and their children.

—**Jennifer Kramer**, MA, LPC

Is This Domestic Abuse?

Is This Domestic Abuse?

*A Handbook for Christian Women
Who Feel Hopeless in Their Marriage*

REBECCA COMMEAN

STONEBROOK
PUBLISHING

Stonebrook Publishing
Saint Louis, Missouri

STONEBROOK PUBLISHING

A STONEBROOK PUBLISHING BOOK
©2023 Rebecca Commean

All rights reserved. Published in the United States by Stonebrook Publishing, a division of Stonebrook Enterprises, LLC, Saint Louis, Missouri. No part of this book may be reproduced, scanned, or distributed in any printed or electronic form without written permission from the author.

Please do not participate in or encourage piracy of copyrighted materials in violation of the author's rights.

Scripture taken from the New King James Version®.
Copyright © 1982 by Thomas Nelson. Used by permission.
All rights reserved.

Library of Congress Control Number: 2023914683

Paperback ISBN: 978-1-955711-29-6
eBook ISBN: 978-1-955711-30-2

www.stonebrookpublishing.net
PRINTED IN THE UNITED STATES OF AMERICA

This book is dedicated to:

Gunther, who absolutely terrified me as a child.
Mr. G and his sons, who I believe sexually molested me as a young girl.
Carl P, who I bullied in fifth grade for no reason other than what I was experiencing.
Peter, who I beat up in seventh grade because he hit Kim too hard, one too many times.
Dan E, who bullied me mercilessly for all four years of high school.
My parents and all my grandparents, who grew up with traumas children should not have to endure.

All these people have suffered. We have all suffered and have inflicted suffering on others because of our own. For the part I have played, I'm deeply sorry. And I hope you can find it in your heart to forgive me. For those who have hurt me, it has made me the person I am now, and for that, I'm grateful. I offer my forgiveness.

This book is also dedicated to my children, who are my brightest hope that goodness and kindness can overcome the darkness of domestic violence. May you shine the light of truth and love in a world so desperately in need.

This book is also dedicated to Steve, Rob, and Scott, true instruments of God, without whom our survival, recovery, and overcoming probably wouldn't have happened. I will be grateful for you and your influence for the rest of my life.

Contents

Preface xi

**PART 1: THE FUNDAMENTALS
OF DOMESTIC ABUSE** 1

1. Types of Domestic Abuse 3
2. Tools Behind the Abuse 18

PART 2: KNOWLEDGE IS POWER 29

3. Arm Yourself with Information 31
4. The Victim's Situation 43
5. Know Thyself 56
6. Help to Heal 68

**PART 3: DOMESTIC ABUSE AND THE
LEGAL SYSTEM** 77

7. Problems in Our Legal System 79
8. Solutions for Our Legal System 91

PART 4: DOMESTIC ABUSE AND THE CHURCH...101

9. What Does God Say About Domestic Violence? 103
10. What Does the Church Believe About Domestic Violence?....................128
11. Standard Doctrinal Statements and the Role of the Clergy............................140
12. What Does the Church Need to Do Now? 149

PART 5: ESCAPE AND RECOVERY FROM DOMESTIC VIOLENCE 159

13. Options/Safety Planning......................161
14. The Children 197
15. Going Forward in Empowerment................221

Resources 231
    The Internet 231
    Federal Resources 232
    State Resources 233
    Missouri Resources 233

Further Reading 249

Acknowledgments................................251

About the Author 253

Preface

Have you ever talked with someone and they casually mentioned they were being abused by their partner at home? Do co-workers ever tell you they're staying at a domestic violence shelter? How many people at church talk about their domestic violence situations? Domestic Violence, also called Intimate Partner Violence or Domestic Abuse, affects vast numbers of people, but we rarely, if ever, hear about it in our inner circles.

For twenty-five years, I thought I was in a Christian marriage. All that time, I thought my husband loved me and my children; he was just an unhappy person. For twenty-five years, I thought domestic violence meant getting beaten up—not the confusing, despairing, never-good-enough life I was living. I didn't know that the problem was *not me* for twenty-five years. For twenty-five years, I never considered that what I lived with was abusive. When I finally got bold enough to tell my pastor, he told me that "domestic violence" and "abuse" were words that didn't appear in Scripture; therefore, there was no such thing.

Only after I became suicidal and sought counseling did I begin to realize the truth of my situation. Once I understood, I wanted to ensure that no other wife would suffer twenty-five years of abuse before she finally understood its treachery. This book is the fruit of my years of ignorance and my research, study, and awakening that's occurred since then.

Would it surprise you that about 1/3 of women and 1/7 of men are victims of physical or sexual abuse?[1] That also means that 1/3 of men and 1/7 of women are abusers. Combining those numbers represents nearly 50 percent of the adult population. In studies that isolated *emotional abuse*, close to 50 percent of men and women reported they had experienced it. That's an astounding number of people.

This book will not only educate you on what domestic violence is and what you need to know to overcome it—or help someone immersed in it—but also show you *why* domestic violence is so catastrophic. This is your call to arms. You will know the truth. Domestic violence occurs all around you, and it's time to do something about it.

I asked my pastor if I could make a presentation for our denominational leadership about domestic violence. We had a profitable discussion about the scourge of domestic violence in the community and the church. I asserted that churches don't have a clue about how to handle domestic violence, and he agreed. He said he'd ask the local/district leadership about my presentation the next time they met. After a few weeks, I'd heard nothing, so I approached him after service.

"What did you find out about my presentation?" I asked.

He shook his head. "I broached the subject, and the leadership asked me about your credentials on this subject."

The implication was that I only had something valid to say if I had the proper educational background. Who else but a victim would have the experience to share? So, I'm telling you my story—you, who may well recognize yourself in my words.

---

[1] World Health Organization, "Devastatingly pervasive: 1 in 3 women globally experience violence" 9 March 2021, and National Domestic Violence Hotline, "Domestic Violence Statistics," https://www.who.int/news/item/09-03-2021-devastatingly-pervasive-1-in-3-women-globally-experience-violence.

IS THIS DOMESTIC ABUSE?

I FELL IN LOVE. I was in college, and he came to fix our high-tech scanner. He was intelligent and funny, had a good job, and earned a good living. He had a nice car and seemed just as smitten with me as I was with him. He grew up in church, which was essential to me because I had, too. As our relationship developed, I learned he came from an abusive home. That didn't bother me. I thought we could get through his past together and create a better life in our marriage with our family. I could see my husband needed help. He needed safety, security, love, and respect. And I thought he could overcome his demons if I gave him those things. That's not what happened.

We got married in 1990 and had nine children and three miscarriages. As time passed, he despised me more and more. I remember when he berated me and said I wasn't good at anything.

I was crying and terribly hurt, but I said, "I know I'm a good mother."

He curled his lip and shrugged his shoulders. "Well, that just shows how stupid you are."

He wasn't physically violent very often. Instead, he used his words, or the lack thereof, with devastating effect. When I went to the church for help, they told me I needed to submit more and be a better wife.

They asked, "Are you sure you're a Christian?"

After twenty-five years, I'd lived through his extramarital affair; things I'd seen him do to my girls that made me very, very uncomfortable; ever-escalating verbal, emotional, and physical abuse; as well as sexual, spiritual, and financial abuse—all of which I didn't know how to recognize. I was tormented day and night, confused, despairing, entirely without hope, filled with desperation, and suicidal. After weeks of prayer and fasting, I decided to file for divorce. Though my church elders told me I had Biblical grounds, they also told me:

"God hates divorce."

"Remember Nineva and Hosea."

"If you go through with this, you'll lose all rights to your children. They'll all be taken away."

In hindsight, I now see that my church elders were complicit in my abuse. Much later, I read that abusers frequently threaten to take the children away to force their partners to stay. My elders were trying to force me to stay in the marriage by threatening me with losing my children. I thought they were being honest about the risk rather than manipulating me to force me to submit to more abuse.

Despite that threat, I filed for divorce. I'd been warned by a women's court advocate that I would get nowhere. The courts don't listen in cases of domestic violence; they only pay attention to the one who has the money, and since I'd always been a stay-at-home mom to nine children, homeschooling since 2001, that sure wasn't me. She said my best alternative was to stay in the marriage and try to protect the children from the inside.

I refused to believe the courts could be so callous to injustice and abuse. But she was right. The courts considered making my second-oldest daughter the "surrogate mother" while my husband had 50 percent custody. Since my youngest child was about seven, that would force her into servitude under my abusive husband for the next ten years of her life. I couldn't do that to her, and I couldn't allow him to have 50 percent unsupervised custody of my children. So, I did what the women's advocate had suggested initially. I dropped the case and stayed in the marriage, determined to fight from within.

Everything instantly became exponentially worse. Can you fathom what it's like to live with twenty-five years of all manner of abuse, take your abuser to court, then give up and go back to being married and living in the same house? I'd embarrassed him publicly, and the judge asserted that what was wrong was that "I just wanted a little more freedom than I did when I first got married, didn't I?" The courts had validated my husband's behavior.

After a couple of months, I decided to focus on something new. I reached out to a family friend and spent hours reconnecting. During that time, we discovered that while I was wrestling with my issues with my husband, my friend was wrestling with very similar problems with his children, who'd been adopted from overseas. Since we had similar issues, he agreed to act as a mediator between my husband and me. He was the first Christian man who understood, listened, and helped in twenty-five years. He was the first one not charmed by my husband's words or swayed by his lies and deception. He held my husband accountable to the Christian standards my husband said he adhered to. The mediator caught my husband's lies, stood against abuses, and held my husband's feet to the fire.

Interestingly, the mediator contacted my husband after our first conversation to have a weekly Bible study together. They met for several months. I had no idea, and things at home were deteriorating even further. I finally texted the mediator and asked him, "Were you ever able to connect with (my husband)?"

He replied, "Yes. He's been meeting with me every week for Bible study. Why?"

As it turns out, my husband told the mediator that everything was great at home. We were getting along; the children were doing fine—lies, lies, and more lies. He was covering his backside, knowing the mediator would trust him. When I met with the mediator again, the stories I related caused him to think that my husband might have one or more personality disorders. Possibly attachment disorder, possibly narcissistic personality disorder.

Since our mediator was somewhat familiar with these things after dealing with children adopted from traumatic experiences overseas, he started to identify and confront these behaviors in my husband. I spent time researching, thinking, healing, and helping my children heal from their abuses. Our mediator completely reversed the financial abuse by turning the household finances over to me, and he miraculously negotiated the departure of my husband from our home after discovering he'd been lying to both of us—once again—for over a year about thousands of dollars.

Our mediator introduced accountability into the picture, which has been the most tremendous blessing from God. Since the only communication my husband and I have is in writing—with our mediator copied on all communications—my husband is forced to choose between being abusive toward me and looking good enough to be respected by an outside party. Looking good to other people is critical to managing his abusive behaviors.

The church leadership's original question was, "What are your credentials?" I don't have a degree in domestic violence. But I've lived with it, experienced it, and overcome it. That's it. I'm an overcomer. My nine children are overcomers. Together we are healing, learning, growing, and going above and beyond. And now you can, too.

PART 1

The Fundamentals of Domestic Abuse

1

Types of Domestic Abuse

When thinking about domestic abuse, most people think of physical violence: bruised and battered women and children. Indeed, abuse of this nature happens way too much. But there's so much more to physical abuse than inflicting bodily injury. Physical abuse also inflicts pain or injury to something or someone important to you. Many abusers will destroy clothing, harm pets, and discard or damage sentimental possessions or items of value to abuse and intimidate the victim. They'll threaten or harm children, family members, or friends. Abusers will also be physically intimidating and punch holes in a wall, brandish weapons, or tower over a victim in rage, causing great fear in the victim.

Physical Abuse

Physical abuse is anything that could endanger or cause harm—withholding food or water, refusing medical attention, and refusing to allow others to freely come and go as they please fall into this category. The Turpin family in California is an excellent example. They chained their children, restricted access to food and water, didn't allow them to use the toilet, and made them live in filth. Even if they never actually injured the children, they certainly harmed them physically. More information about this case can be seen in the Netflix documentary *Children of God, Escape from a House of Horror* on ABC or Hulu, and *The Turpin 13: Family Secrets Exposed* on Amazon Prime.

Physical abuse is anything that could endanger or cause harm.

This case particularly triggered me because religion played such a crucial role. The Turpins were Pentecostal, which was my husband's religion. The mother, Louise, was a preacher's daughter, yet she'd been sex-trafficked by her mother. The horrific use of religion to justify behavior, cover up wrongdoing, hide behind, and make a façade for the world to see is so sickening—and not altogether uncommon.

Sexual Abuse

Sexual abuse is another kind of domestic violence. My husband told me that God told him we would have more children. Yet, we rarely had sex. I told him that we probably needed to have sex for that to happen and that I was here, in part, for precisely that purpose. Then one day, he told me that he'd only said that God told him we'd have more children, so I'd be more interested in sex. In the next breath, he told me that God told him he needed to give up sex. These manipulative and contradictory statements constitute a part of sexual abuse.

Sometimes people wonder how there can be sexual abuse between intimate partners. Just because you're in an intimate relationship doesn't mean there's no need for mutual consent! Yes, rape does occur in marriage. Abusers may drug and rape their partners when they're sick, injured, recuperating from serious illness, or undergoing surgical procedures or chemotherapy. Sexual abuse is anything one partner forces on another. It's withholding or refusing sexual contact as well as too much, unusual, or unwanted sexual activity, like making one partner have sex with multiple partners, videoing them during sex, or using objects on another person when they don't want that. Using restraints, inflicting pain or injury, or going beyond a partner's set limits or boundaries is sexual abuse. Trading one person to another for sex for money is sexual abuse and is called prostitution/pimping or sex trafficking. If there's no mutual consent, it's sexual abuse.

When my husband told me we would have more children, but God told him not to have sex, I was furious at his manipulation. At that point, I could deal with him lying all the time. But telling me a lie and getting God involved was beyond what I could take.

Sobbing, I called my elder's wife. "I'm handing him over to Satan," I told her.

"I don't think you can do that," she said.

"I looked it up," I replied. "There are two instances in Scripture. In one case, it's a group of people that hands someone over to Satan, and in the other, it's just one person. So, I think I can."

I could not bear to see the man, let alone submit to anything intimate. I could not think about it without getting physically sick. Shaking and embarrassed one Sunday morning, I pulled aside my church elder and my husband.

"The Bible says not to deprive one another except for prayer and fasting. I would like to request a time of prayer and fasting." I included the elder because I knew if I simply told my husband, he'd refuse. But if the elder was included and didn't think it was unreasonable, my husband would have to agree.

"For how long?" they asked.

"I don't know," I said. "I don't know how long it will take to get my answer." They kept pressing for a date, so I finally said, "Maybe four to six weeks."

What do you know? Suddenly, my husband was ravenous for sex. He asked me every day when my fast would be over. We usually went months between sexual encounters. Months. In fact, the last time we'd had sex had been twenty-seven months earlier. The bottom line was *control*. He deprived us of a sexual relationship until I decided to ask for a fast. Then he couldn't wait for the fast to be over.

Emotional Abuse

A third type of domestic violence is *emotional, psychological, or mental abuse*. While these terms can be interchangeable, I believe emotional abuse has more to do with your feelings; psychological abuse involves mental processes involving decisions or conclusions; mental abuse involves manipulating facts. But they all deal with what's going on in your head. On VeryWellMind.com, emotional abuse is defined as "using emotions to criticize, embarrass, shame, blame, or otherwise manipulate another person. In general, a relationship is emotionally abusive when a consistent pattern of abusive words and bullying behaviors wear down a person's self-esteem and undermine their mental health."

> *Emotional abuse has more to do with your feelings; psychological abuse involves mental processes involving decisions or conclusions; mental abuse involves manipulating facts.*

According to the National Network to End Domestic

IS THIS DOMESTIC ABUSE?

Violence, "The underlying goal of emotional abuse is to control the victim by discrediting, isolating, and silencing." Ultimately, the victim feels trapped, too wounded to endure the relationship any longer, and too afraid to leave. So, the cycle repeats itself.

The desire to control is always behind any type of abuse, but emotional abuse can take some mind-bending forms. This is what makes emotional abuse so destructive. While emotional abuse leaves no visible wounds, it affects victims for the rest of their lives and damages children, grandchildren, and even friends and acquaintances. How? An emotional abuser has several strategies that cause their target to question their sanity. Professionals refer to these strategies as gaslighting, projection, blame-shifting, crazymaking, and the good, old-fashioned bald-faced lie. Each method creates confusion in the victim's mind and causes them to question reality. This instability gives the abuser control over the situation. They use verbal threats, humiliating remarks, condescending tones, and statements designed to make the victim feel stupid and worthless. They will insult, publicly humiliate, put down, sabotage the victim's efforts and labor, harass them, say and do conflicting things, even contradictory things, all in a deliberate attempt to confuse, belittle, and destroy the victim's self-worth, confidence, and rational thought. Increasingly, the victim doubts themself and their worth and abilities, while the abuser gains more and more control over greater aspects of the victim's life. In the end, the victim feels hopelessness and despair while being completely isolated from family, friends, acquaintances, and people at work (if they even had a job). They're wholly trapped.

The desire to control is always behind any type of abuse, but emotional abuse can take some mind-bending forms.

Post-Traumatic Stress Disorder (PTSD) is common among long-term emotional and other domestic abuse victims. Low self-esteem and confidence impair the victim's ability to function well and achieve as a productive member of society. Depression keeps victims from being productive, happy, thriving, and reaching their full potential. Anxiety keeps them from the happiness and joy of discovering new things and pushing themselves to greater heights. Victims cannot heal until contact with the abuser is halted, and it takes a long time to recover from the years of mental anguish. The vestiges and remnants of that abuse linger long after escape from the abusive relationship.

MY HUSBAND WAS SO MUCH LIKE HIS MOTHER. When he was growing up, she wanted the house to be perfectly clean. Her children had to do the cleaning, and they had to do it exactly right. He hated that and harbored ill will toward her for her entire life.

I was not like his mother. I was not, nor ever will be, a perfectionistic housekeeper. After all, we had nine children. We had clutter and dirty dishes but no hoarding or pest infestations aside from the occasional fleas on pets. The garbage was removed. Chores were done. Healthy meals were prepared. Schoolwork was done. The laundry was always behind, but everybody had clean clothes to wear. When I said I wanted to try planting a garden, my husband told me for the umpteenth time what a terrible housekeeper I was. How could I keep up with a garden if I could not manage laundry, dishes, etc.? I couldn't do it, I wasn't capable of doing it, and anything I would try would be a total failure.

I learned about composting, square-foot gardening, companion planting, etc. When he finally agreed to let me plant a garden, I set it up the way I'd learned. I took him down and showed him everything I was doing and why.

"That's the stupidest thing I've ever heard of," he scoffed and went on and on about all the things that were stupid about it. About a week later, a neighbor down the road who was a master gardener stopped by to see the garden. My husband happened to be home, and our neighbor started talking about all the things I'd done right and why those things were beneficial. My husband was all smiles and nods.

"Isn't that amazing?" he said to me. "We should be doing that."

He repeated that even after the master gardener told him what I did right. My husband still acted like I wasn't doing those things, even though it was clear that I was.

Financial Abuse

A fourth type of abuse is *financial abuse*. Financial abuse can take many forms, but the outcome is always the same—the victim has no control over the money. Milder forms of financial abuse may be that the victim has no knowledge of any household financial matters. Perhaps the victim is given an allowance for certain monthly needs, but the rest of the money is kept secret by the abuser. The abuser has the final say on anything and everything that's purchased, which is often used as a weapon against the victim. Anything the victim needs or wants is too expensive, but anything the abuser needs or wants is affordable—no matter how extravagant. Or perhaps the abuser is frugal to the point of neglecting the others in the family.

Financial abuse doesn't stop there. Perhaps the abuser can't hold down a job but insists on

Financial abuse can take many forms, but the outcome is always the same—the victim has no control over the money.

playing video games or going out with friends all day instead of job hunting. When the bills are due, it's the victim's fault that there's no money to pay them. I have a friend whose husband quit his job because he didn't like it. He then spent so much time at a McDonald's playing video games online that the seat he used was noticeably and substantially more worn than any of the other seats in the restaurant.

Meanwhile, my friend was a stay-at-home, homeschooling mother of six children. Since he only played video games, the money ran out quickly. She sold homeschool materials and did other work from home to try to pay bills. Her husband enjoyed the benefits of the income but refused to contribute to the financial success of the household.

More than one woman I know has a husband who suddenly quits working because he doesn't want to work anymore. The wives search for job opportunities to present to them, but they aren't interested. Or they go to the interview but do poorly on purpose. Or they even get offered a job but turn it down. One friend put her children in public school instead of continuing to homeschool and got a job to provide for the family. Her husband stayed home and did nothing, not even taking care of minor repairs or lawn mowing. This is also financial abuse.

The abuser may sabotage the victim's employment, prevent the victim from earning a wage, or they may confiscate the victim's income. The abuser may harass the victim at work so much that the victim gets fired, but since the abuser refuses to find a job, there's no income at all. Then the victim gets blamed because she got fired.

I have a friend who emigrated from Mexico with her husband. After they arrived and were both employed, the husband told her that all wives pay rent to their husbands in America. So, he charged her several hundred dollars a month in rent. The bottom line is that the abuser controls the situation, and the victim is financially unable to leave the relationship or have any say in financial matters.

In my situation, my husband handled the bills for the first several years; then I handled the bills. I worked hard to budget and track expenses. Since my husband didn't pay the bills, I think he felt completely free with spending. I was always a stay-at-home mom, and we agreed I wouldn't spend money unless I cleared it with him first. After several years of this, we didn't have enough income to pay for everything every month. So, he took over the bill paying.

We'd established that I spent about $1,000 per month on groceries. He gave me $1,000 each month, and that's all I had to get food for the family. The problem was that we had five children at the time, and I didn't get a raise for well over ten years, although we'd added another four children. Furthermore, any medicine or doctor visits came from my grocery allowance, as did gas for my vehicle, toiletries, cleaning supplies, clothes and shoes for the children, etc. I seldom bought clothes or shoes for myself; I couldn't make $1,000 stretch that far. Thrift store shopping twice a year on 50-percent-off-days supplied the nine children with what they needed for the most part. That, too, is financial abuse.

When I filed for divorce, my husband took all the money out of our joint account and left me with $8.32 to cover the monthly expenses for our kids and me. The following month, he gave me $400. While we were in court, I figured I needed $2,500 per month to support the family. The judge agreed and said I should get between $3,000 and $4,000 per month.

After I dropped the charges, my husband raised my allowance to $1,300 a month. Fortunately, when the mediator

> *When I filed for divorce, my husband took all the money out of our joint account and left me with $8.32 to take care of the monthly expenses for our kids and me.*

got involved, reviewed the history, and saw that my husband had let certain bills slide, he insisted that the financial matters be turned over to me. While it was an added stress to also be responsible for the mortgage, utilities, and other bills, the relief of being able to use *all* the monthly income for *the family's needs* was wonderful. It was so good to know everything would be taken care of properly.

Spiritual Abuse

Put bluntly, *spiritual abuse* is a horrible evil plague cloaked in the most self-righteous, judgmental, non-Biblical, pious-sounding, meaningless platitudes. There is no good, polite, or politically correct way to discuss it. Why? All other forms of abuse have one abuser and one victim. With spiritual abuse, there is one victim, one intimate partner abuser, and a whole host of Christian (or other religious affiliation) enablers and abusers who are completely ignorant of the dynamics of an abusive situation. They give "religiously sound" advice that forces victims to accept responsibility for the abuse and stay in it—even though doing so is contrary to the Bible, from Genesis to Revelation.

The religious community has much responsibility in this appalling situation. Still, most clergy and spiritual authority figures either do not—or will not—understand the role the church is currently playing or what it needs to do instead. Since my knowledge is limited to those who profess Jesus Christ as Lord, my comments have that foundation. If you are of a different religious group, you know the doctrinal beliefs, so you can apply this to your situation.

You must know for yourself what God says about domestic violence, not what your clergyman *says* that God says. You must also ensure that you are appropriating Scripture as it was intended. You need to evaluate what the Scripture truly says about domestic violence. It differs greatly from what most clergy or Biblical teachers advise you. (More about this in Part 4 of this book.)

For our purposes, spiritual abuse would be if a husband says or does something mean, hateful, or harmful to his wife, then says, "You're supposed to submit to me." Or if a husband is financially, verbally, sexually, physically, or emotionally abusive, and the wife goes to her pastor, who asks if the husband is providing for the family's physical needs. If she answers, "Yes," and the pastor concludes that he's fulfilling his obligation and that she should be content and grateful for his provision, that's spiritual abuse. Or . . .

- The pastor says you need to be careful not to allow a root of bitterness to grow
- The pastor says that you need to forgive, bless, and honor your husband
- The pastor says the ever-present counsel of so many in Christendom: "You know, God hates divorce"

. . . all the while leaving the abuse itself left unaddressed.

Yes, those things are in Scripture, so why are they a problem? They're a problem because they're not what God says about *domestic violence*. God says to protect the oppressed. (Scriptures teach this principle over and over, and God Himself protected David from Saul.) The church says the oppressed need to continue in it. God says oppressors are to be punished (Cain and Abel), and the church says to act like nothing happened and pray. God says for wives to respect their husbands and for men to love their

You must know for yourself what God says about domestic violence, not what your clergyman says that God says.

partners. The church says wives are to respect their husbands, and if the man is not loving, it's because she's not respectful. Therefore, she deserves his response and better start respecting him. What the church counsels, in many cases, is terribly harmful because it doesn't address the abuse. It only addresses the victim and what she's doing wrong.

This will not solve the problem. It often worsens the problem because it supports the abuser in his abusive treatment and upholds the "right" of the man to be the "head of the home." While male victims don't have the "submit to your head" teaching to deal with, they're still subject to all the other Scriptural doctrines that the church misapplies to domestic violence situations.

I was told repeatedly to turn the other cheek and to bless, not curse. I was reminded of the passage in Matthew that tells us to love our enemies and pray for those who persecute us. The problem is that the passage refers to our enemies—unbelievers who mistreat us *for Christ's sake.* The passage is NOT referring to our spouses. If a victim goes to their pastor and the pastor refers to this passage, the pastor has just confirmed the abuser is an unbeliever, a wolf in sheep's clothing, a false prophet. And what do the Scriptures tell us about wolves in sheep's clothing? Matthew 7:19 says, "Every tree that does not bear good fruit is cut down and thrown into the fire." Second Peter, chapter 2 is perhaps the most terrifying passage regarding false prophets in the Scriptures. If this is indeed the case, should not the unbelieving, wolf, false, abusive spouse be the one corrected by the pastor, not the victim of the abuse? I Corinthians 6 says:

> Do not be unequally yoked together with unbelievers. For what fellowship has righteousness with lawlessness? And what communion has light with darkness? And what accord has Christ with Belial? Or what part has a believer with an unbeliever? And what agreement has the temple of God

with idols? For you are the temple of the living God. God has said: "I will dwell in them and walk among them. I will be their God, and they shall be my people. Therefore, come out from among them and be separate," says the Lord. "Do not touch what is unclean, and I will receive you. I will be a Father to you, and you shall be My sons and daughters," says the Lord Almighty.

If a pastor references Matthew 5, the entire Sermon on the Mount speaks about our interactions with unbelievers, evil ones, or enemies. Therefore, the pastor equates the abuser with unbelievers, evildoers, and enemies. Does it not stand to reason, then, that I Corinthians 6 should be the standard passage when dealing with abuse cases? "Do not be unequally yoked with unbelievers . . . Do not touch what is unclean, and I will receive you."

Verbal Abuse

The final recognized form of domestic violence is *verbal abuse*. This is probably the most common—and least recognized—of all the abuse types. When anyone yells at their spouse or significant other; when they swear at them or tell them they're stupid; when they're harsh or critical or condemning or just plain mean with their words, that is verbal abuse. Anything that is not kind, controlled, helpful, true, and worded nicely is verbal abuse. Volume does not make things abusive or not abusive. If someone shouts at their spouse and calls them a stupid $% $ %$*&^ who can never do anything right, and another whispers it in their partner's ear, are the words—or the intent—any less abusive? Of course not.

The following acronym can help determine if your words are abusive or not. Your answers should be *yes* to all the questions. Something may be true, but if it's not kind, then don't say it.

> **Before You Speak: THINK**
> T: Is it *true?*
> H: Is it *helpful?*
> I: Is it *inspiring?*
> N: Is it *necessary?*
> K: Is it *kind?*

The problem with verbal abuse is that it comes from someone you love and who you believe loves you. If you hear something often enough, you'll believe it, whether true or not. Verbal abusers use words to tear down their victims. They call them names, tell them they aren't any good, and phrase things in a way that makes them feel stupid. Criticizing and condemning, they can never be pleased or happy. There's always something to complain about, always something to make them grumpy. And they always have an excuse: They had a bad day. They're stressed. It's someone else's fault. The children are irritating. Somebody left their tools out. The house is messy. They didn't get sex when they wanted it, etc.

Verbal abusers use words to tear down their victims.

Verbal abuse is often combined with emotional abuse, which makes matters even worse. Now, the victim is not only condemned, criticized, and shouted at, but the victim is also blamed for the whole episode, told lies to gaslight them, and ends up feeling like they're going insane and that their abuser is the victim.

Just because someone you love says bad things doesn't make them true. Just because you love someone doesn't mean they love you, which is demonstrated by the words that come out of their mouths. Just because you love someone doesn't mean they're telling you the truth, they care about your feelings, or they're good for you to be around. You need to love yourself. If someone loves you, they won't tear you down with their words. If their words are abusive, they don't love you.

The six forms of domestic violence encompass every facet of life. There's no safe place. Our minds and hearts, our workplaces and churches, our money, and our time, what we see and hear—every facet of our lives is touched by abuse when the abuser is in the home. We orchestrate our whole lives around avoiding it.

It's time to stop accommodating your abuser and start liberating yourself; stop appeasing and start countering. Stop being a victim and start on the path to being an overcomer.

2

Tools Behind the Abuse

Abusers have a complete bag of tricks to dominate and control their victims. Among them are:

- Manipulation
- Gaslighting/crazymaking
- Stockholm Syndrome
- Lies and deception
- Control and jealousy
- Blame shifting
- Intimidation and threats
- Vindictiveness
- Mental illness

Understanding the tricks that abusers use helps you to see abuses as they're happening and helps you to counter them by simply changing your reactions and responses. Changing yourself is the first step in overcoming, and to change yourself appropriately, you need to know what you are up against.

In the Chapter 1 section on emotional abuse, I listed some terms that probably are not too familiar: manipulation, gaslighting/crazymaking, and Stockholm Syndrome. Let's take a deeper look.

Manipulation

Manipulation is getting anybody to do anything without directly asking, telling, or explaining what is desired, then trying to trick the victim into thinking the desired outcome was their idea. For example, if a child wants to do an activity and the parent doesn't want the child to do this, they could say no, explain why, and be done. They could also have a discussion where the parent explains their thinking, so the child can follow the reasoning and understand the final decision.

Or the parent could consider what thought process would lead the child to determine the activity was not a good idea on their own, and fabricate something to cause the child to decide the activity isn't a good plan—so the parent doesn't have to say no. This is manipulation.

A manipulator will lie, deceive, leave out vital information, leave impressions, suggest, drop innuendos, and do whatever is necessary to get the other person to make the decision the abuser wants without the abuser saying it. Why is this manipulation bad? Because it's not about persuasion or getting the other to understand your argument to agree with you. It's only about the manipulator controlling the victim and using whatever tactics are necessary to achieve that end. This usually means some form of verbal and emotional abuse. Manipulation is used to take advantage of another, control another, escape responsibility, and elevate oneself over another.

Gaslighting and Crazymaking

Gaslighting and crazymaking are deliberate campaigns to get the victim to doubt their perception of reality. Doubting your knowledge of the truth—of reality—causes confusion and makes you question your sanity. How can someone create so much doubt about your life that you feel like you're losing your mind? When they're successful, it brings both amusement and a sense of almighty power to the abusive partner.

Here's a hypothetical example: Say you're working in the kitchen, and when you leave, you turn off the light and go to another room down the hall. Your abuser, in the living room, gets up, turns the light on, and sits back down. When you return to the room an hour later, you're sure you turned off the light, but you see it's on. So, you ask your abuser if he turned on the light, and he says that you never turned it off. You turn it off again and say, "You are my witness. I turned off the light!" After you leave, he gets up again, turns on the light, and returns to his seat. You go back an hour or two later, and the light is on. You say, "Hey! I know I turned off the light. You are my witness." Then he says that he doesn't know anything about it. That light has been on all day.

You, surprised and flustered, know you turned it off. No one else is there, and he saw you turn it off. You say again that he saw you turn off the light. Now your abuser gets upset. He says he's been waiting for you to turn it off because he's sick and tired of being the only one responsible to save money on the electric bill, and it's about time you learned to turn the %&#*@ light off! You're the problem in the relationship here, not him.

Most of the time, gaslighting and crazymaking are interchangeable terms. Both get their power from your willingness to believe the best about people and trust their sincerity. You want to believe that your partner is trustworthy and honest.

You love your partner and don't want to do anything that might damage the relationship. You empathize with your partner, so you back off. Perhaps you're just not remembering correctly. Perhaps you just *thought* you turned off the light. You had no idea your partner felt pressure about the electric bill, and you feel terrible that your partner thinks you're irresponsible.

So, you apologize to your abuser, who's adopted a posture of righteous indignation. He storms off without a word and unleashes the full force of the silent treatment. The silent treatment continues for some time—days or even weeks—while you try to make amends, apologize repeatedly, can't understand why this is lasting so long, and wonder what you can do to get things back to normal again. As this becomes a pattern in life, you never know which reality is right—your version or his.

Maybe now you can begin to understand the back-and-forth distress that happens in

> *The more it happens, the more the victim feels they're going insane. And that's very scary.*

someone who's being emotionally abused. If there's any doubt or confusion in the victim's mind, the abuser controls the relationship. And they won't hesitate to use more gaslighting or crazymaking at every opportunity. The more it happens, the more the victim feels insane. And that's very scary.

Stockholm Syndrome

And now about Stockholm Syndrome, which is defined by britannica.com in the following way:

> Psychologists who have studied the syndrome believe that the bond is initially created when a captor threatens a captive's life, deliberates, and then chooses not to kill the

captive. The captive's relief at the removal of the death threat is transposed into feelings of gratitude toward the captor for giving him or her life... The survival instinct is at the heart of the Stockholm syndrome. *Victims live in enforced dependence and interpret rare or small acts of kindness amid horrible conditions as good treatment. They often become hypervigilant to the needs and demands of their captors, making psychological links between the captors' happiness and their own.* Indeed, the syndrome is marked not only by a positive bond between captive and captor but also by a negative attitude on behalf of the captive toward authorities who threaten the captor-captive relationship.
(Italics mine.)

This, in a nutshell, describes the life of the victim of domestic abuse. Stockholm Syndrome explains why many women feel loyalty, affection, and trust toward their abuser. It also explains why they frequently won't press charges against him when it's warranted. They've been brainwashed into believing that this relationship is the best, or the only one, they'll ever have or that their abuser is their savior.

Lies and Deception

Another hallmark of an abusive relationship is that the abuser is deceitful about almost everything—even things they don't need to falsify. And since we don't want to believe that our partner would lie to us, we accept what they say as the truth. Even when we have evidence that they're lying, covering up something, or omitting a key fact, we bend our minds into whatever contortion is necessary to make their lies seem plausible. They know this and use it to their advantage. Outright lies, omission of information leading to erroneous beliefs, deception, misleading statements, and letting you think something is the truth when they know it isn't are all part of the arsenal designed to keep the victim confused. The abuser gains power by confusing the victim.

What's baffling is the great lengths the abuser goes to in order to convince others that they're telling the truth and can be trusted, sometimes keeping up the facade—or multiple facades—for weeks, months, and even years. I suspect a thrill and a twisted pride are associated with how long a lie appears to be the truth and how many people can be duped. I believe it strokes the abuser's ego. Rarely, if ever, does the abuser show any kind of remorse, nor do they admit any wrongdoing. If anything, they may be irritated that the lie was uncovered because they now must begin a new deception about something else.

Another hallmark of an abusive relationship is that the abuser is deceitful about almost everything—even things they don't need to falsify.

Control and Jealousy

Nearly all domestic violence has at its root the need to control and the violent jealousy of anything and everything that infringes on that control. The basis of any intimate relationship should be love. Are control and love the same thing? The self-control required for any healthy relationship is swapped for the need to control the victim. When the perpetrator displays jealousy, they're not jealous because they desire you and your time and affection. They're jealous of the threat to their control over you. Early in a relationship, the victim will often feel special or honored by the jealousy shown by the abuser. But it doesn't improve over time. Jealousy and control escalate, getting more intense, threatening, and violent. It becomes life-threatening.

Blame-Shifting and Projection

Blame-shifting and projection are two ways a perpetrator tries to shift responsibility for anything undesirable onto the victim. Blame-shifting and projection are different in that blame-shifting takes the blame for something off the abuser and puts it on the victim. In contrast, projection is the feelings, fears, emotions, motivations, attitudes, or characteristics of the abuser being verbally thrust upon the victim. An example of blame shifting is if a man tells his wife that he's going to mow the lawn, then sometime later in the day, starts yelling at her that he can't mow the lawn because she didn't get the mower serviced, and she should know to get it serviced during the winter so he can use it. An example of projection is if he still hasn't mowed the lawn sometime later in the day and starts complaining to her about how she never gets anything done. She procrastinates about everything and is always lazy. He just can't stand that about her. That's projection.

We were rehabbing our family room into a large bedroom for our four oldest daughters. All the drywall had been removed, new insulation put in, new drywall put up, and the arduous task of gooping and sanding was in full swing. I had just finished gooping around the French doors when my husband innocently picked something up off the floor and leaned against the door frame for support. His hand and arm were covered with fresh goop, and big finger dents were in the goop on the wall.

"Ahh," he groaned.

I stood up from my work and looked. I smiled at him. I thought it was funny and an easy mistake to make. I did it all the time, and I was the one gooping!

IS THIS DOMESTIC ABUSE?

Nearly shouting at me, he said, "I'm sorry! I'm sorry, OK? I'm sorry!"

Confused and taken aback, I said, "I smiled at you."

"When you smile at me, I don't know if you're happy or mad!"

I was so upset I went outside, got in the car, and went for a drive. He doesn't know whether a smile means I'm happy or mad. Why must a funny situation be turned into me being a bad guy? I was not aggravated, upset, mad, or anything of the sort, yet he acted like I was tearing his head off, and he was the victim. Projection, gaslighting, and blame-shifting are all tactics of an abuser.

A clear illustration of both blame shifting and projection—along with lies and deception—can be seen in a prominent case from 2018: the case of Shanann Watts. Shanann Watts and her two little girls disappeared and were later found dead. Shanann was buried in a shallow grave near an oil-storage facility, and her daughters were dumped into crude oil tanks.

Her husband, Christopher Lee Watts, denied involvement and pleaded for their safe return. He denied that he'd been involved in an affair; then, it became obvious that he had been. At first, he said that his family was gone. Then he said he had killed his wife because *she* had strangled one of their daughters. Chris was both blame-shifting and projecting his actions onto his dead wife. In the habit of telling lies, he changed his story multiple times, telling authorities whatever he thought they might believe. Having a wife and daughters inhibited his control over the affair; their presence threatened his control of the situation.

Intimidation and Threats

Intimidation and threats are closely related. While threats can be used to intimidate, an abuser can also intimidate without making any verbal threats. Intimidation includes glaring or maintaining a certain expression on their face; physical actions such as punching the wall or an object, throwing things, or recklessly driving can also be used to intimidate.

> *While threats can be used to intimidate, an abuser can also intimidate without making any verbal threats.*

It was no secret to our tiny church community that our family had some issues, and one day, an elder and his wife had my husband, me, and our four oldest girls sit down in our daughters' bedroom for a discussion. Our elder asked questions of us ladies, and we answered.

After a few questions and answers, my husband said, "You know what," and instantly, we all shut down. That was the end of the conversation.

Our elder said, "Wait a minute. What just happened here? What's going on?"

We knew my husband was saying in no uncertain terms to shut our mouths right now. So, we did.

Threats are verbal—something that's said to control the victim. They can vary in intention, sometimes attempting to instill fear, sometimes designed to make the victim feel stupid, ashamed, or embarrassed. Again, the whole purpose is control. If the abuser can make the victim afraid to disagree by acting physically threatening, that's what they'll do. If the abuser can get the victim to do what they want by making the victim feel stupid, that's what they'll do. Their whole objective is to control their victim's thoughts, words, and actions, and they'll do it by whatever means they can.

Vindictiveness

Many times, vindictiveness is a motivation behind domestic violence. Why would an abuser seek to exact revenge if the victim is, in fact, innocent in the relationship? Perpetrators of domestic violence do not think or act in ways that are logical or make sense to those who understand the components of healthy relationships. Things that wouldn't matter in a healthy relationship can be very important and become personal affronts and insults to the perpetrator.

For example, if a child doesn't use a Kleenex folded in the same manner as the perpetrator, they might feel the child is disrespectful or rebellious and deserving of punishment. In contrast, in a normal relationship, the child can use the Kleenex however they want. My children were spanked for not using a Kleenex "correctly." I stopped buying facial tissues.

It's virtually impossible for the victim to know and understand everything that will cause the abuser to take revenge. It may vary from day to day—or even within hours. What may be perfectly fine now may be perceived as rebellious and disrespectful later in the evening. Being tired or stressed may affect what's happening, but the basic problem remains: The victim simply cannot know or predict what will cause the abuser to unleash. The fact is that abusers are highly unpredictable and non-sensical. While some circumstances seem to regularly trigger them—like drinking or using drugs—normal everyday existence is full of triggers that nobody can know or predict. That's part of what makes domestic violence so dangerous.

Mental Illness

Domestic violence perpetrators don't think, act, feel, or relate to others in intimate relationships like non-abusive people do. Whether they are diagnosed or not, it's not a stretch to say they're mentally ill.

There was a day when my husband became very angry. I don't remember the details, but he was very angry and said he wanted to make *all* the decisions. So, I called him the next day to ask what he wanted for supper. I tried to reach him repeatedly but never got a hold of him, so I didn't make supper. I figured I could cook after he got home and told me what he wanted. He was very angry when he found out I hadn't made supper.

Domestic violence perpetrators don't think, act, feel, or relate to others in intimate relationships like non-abusive people do.

First, he sidled up next to me and whispered in my ear, "You're going to show me, aren't you? You're just going to show me."

As though I hadn't cooked supper in a deliberate attempt to exact vengeance on him. It was very creepy. I tried to explain that he'd said that he wanted to make all the decisions, so I was trying to do what he said he wanted.

Then he took me upstairs to our bedroom and yelled, "This is stupid! You should know I wasn't talking about the things you normally take care of!"

I again tried to explain that I was trying to do what he said he wanted me to do.

Then he got down on his knees with an angelic smile and said serenely, "Just hit me again. Go ahead and just hit me again."

I hadn't hit him. I'd done what he asked. I felt like he was possessed.

PART 2

Knowledge is Power

3

Arm Yourself with Information

My first step in breaking the cycle of abuse was to stop submitting to my husband (collective gasp from Christendom!). I distinctly remember when my husband said something about our bank accounts. I knew he was lying because I had the bank statements to prove it. So instead of submitting, yielding, and letting it go, I told him he was lying. He denied it, so I got the bank statements and showed him that they proved he was lying. There was nothing he could say.

How can knowledge equate to power when dealing with abusers? Abusers don't act and react like the rest of the world, so it's best to arm yourself with all the information you can and make an informed decision about how you want to live your life. You need knowledge about the following:

- The game
- The statistics
- The lies
- The abuser's background

- The underlying needs
- The abuser's abuse
- The role of drugs and alcohol
- What happens when you try to leave
- What makes an abuser behave

Once you have this knowledge, you can recognize what's happening and why and then take steps to counter, disengage, refuse to enable, and confront in ways that de-escalate, de-fuse, or leave the abuser with no option but to back down.

The first and most important thing you must know is that your life is in danger. So are the lives of your children and your extended family and friends. You are all in danger of being killed. Don't make the mistake of underestimating your abuser or denying that your death is a possibility. You're in danger if you stay, and you're in danger if you leave. The most dangerous time is when you leave. If you choose to stay, the longer you stay, the greater the chances of serious injury or fatality.

> *The first and most important thing you must know is that your life is in danger.*

The Game

So, what do you need to know? First, this is a game. It's a game of strategy, wits, and cunning. It's a mind game. The abuser spends much time studying his victim's reactions, responses, likes, dislikes, what sets her off, what cuts her off, what destroys her, and what woos her back. The perpetrator is like an expert fly fisherman, sending the lure out and reeling in, letting the fish run, then reeling it in repeatedly until the fish is exhausted, confused, and too tired to fight anymore.

IS THIS DOMESTIC ABUSE?

The perpetrator woos his intended victim. The victim has no reason to think he's lying, so she believes his words and accepts his gifts and the nice things he does as true representations of his character. This is what the perpetrator wants. When the victim is well and truly hooked, the perpetrator reels them in.

Cycle of Abuse

1. Tensions Building
Tensions increase, breakdown of communication, victim becomes fearful and feels the need to placate the abuser

2. Incident
Verbal, emotional & physical abuse. Anger, blaming, arguing. Threats. Intimidation.

3. Reconciliation
Abuser apologizes, gives excuses, blames the victim, denies the abuse occurred, or says that it wasn't as bad as the victim claims

4. Calm
Incident is "forgotten", no abuse is taking place. The "honeymoon" phase

This visual from Wikipedia:File:Cycle_of_Abuse.png illustrates the cycle.

The victim, naturally, is confused and upset. What happened to the love of her life? What did she do? What went wrong? She scrambles to figure it out and apologizes, then changes her behavior, word choices, clothes, or whatever. After an undetermined amount of time and for unknown reasons, everything is suddenly fine again. The victim is so relieved that her love is back. The perpetrator demonstrates love for the victim, which makes the victim believe she is right; her guy is a wonderful person. And then, the hook is set again, and the reeling continues.

Each time the trigger may be different. There seems to be no rhyme or reason why you're back in this cycle, but again, the victim scrambles. Each time, the demonstration of love gets less and less, and the reeling in is increasingly painful and confusing.

Trauma bonding and *Stockholm Syndrome* get a strong foothold during this back-and-forth time. The victim is determined to believe the best about their abuser, no matter how bad it gets. The victim equates love with making the abuser happy, i.e., not abusive, maybe even nice on a good day.

The cycle of abuse and enabling creates a never-ending and always escalating pattern that cannot be broken until the victim understands that her behavior contributes to the cycle. The victim must be the one to stop it because the abuser will keep going for the rest of their lives. It's a game. And the victim, once she knows, has the power to stop the game.

You can refuse to play.

The Statistics

According to the Beacon of Hope Crisis Center (beaconofhopeindy.org), the statistics are frightening and appalling. They report:

> Up to 6 million women are believed to be beaten in their homes each year. . . On average, every nine to twelve seconds. Fifty percent of all homeless women and children in America are fleeing domestic violence. Fifty to seventy percent of men who abuse their partners also abuse children in the home. According to the American Medical Association, family violence kills as many women every five years as the total number of Americans who died in the Vietnam War. There are over 20,000 cities and towns in America, but only 1,300 shelters.

It's difficult to get an accurate statistical representation of the impact of domestic violence because there are so many unknown variables. These above statistics pertain to physical violence and do not include sexual, spiritual, emotional, financial, or verbal abuse. Adding in all the other forms of abuse makes the statistics much more sensational.

The Lies

The domestic violence perpetrator is an expert liar. They will lie about anything and everything, even if lying does not benefit them.

I remember when I suggested that we look into getting an external wood furnace with a water heater. Our home was already heated with wood, and I knew that electric water heaters used a lot of electricity. My husband told me that we had a propane water heater. Sometime later, the water heater wasn't heating well, and I asked if the propane tank might be low or empty. Then he said that our water heater was electric. I know next to nothing about water heaters, but I do know they can't be both.

Abusers lie so much and so convincingly that you cannot believe anything they say—good, bad, or indifferent. They lie so much and so convincingly that they seem to believe their lies, even when they contradict themselves. Even when you know they're probably lying, believing what they say is easy because you love them and want to believe your partner.

This is where knowledge is power. You must remove your emotional attachment from the equation. Your emotions, trauma bonding, and Stockholm Syndrome will tell

> *Abusers lie so much and so convincingly that you cannot believe anything they say— good, bad, or indifferent.*

you—scream at you—that you must believe him because you love him, and he loves you. And well-meaning but completely ignorant Christians will tell you, "Love bears all things, believes all things, hopes all things, endures all things! Love never fails!"

But your rational mind must take over. Your rational mind must unemotionally collect data and store it for easy retrieval. You need evidence. That means photos, written documents, copies of emails or texts, social media posts, etc. So, when the perpetrator lies about something, the rational, calm side of you can say, "I know you're lying because of this statement you already made. Either you were lying then, or you are lying now. Either way, I can't believe what you say."

But—you must remember that this is a game, and you must have a strategy. You can't confront your abuser without developing a safety plan, an exit strategy. You must plan to protect yourself and your children as much as possible. Exit strategies are discussed in more detail in Part 5 of this book.

The Abuser's Background

When discussing abusive relationships, people inevitably ask why. Why would someone do that or be that way? Why would a victim accept it? Why doesn't the victim leave? Why would anyone treat someone they love that way? None of it makes any sense.

I don't claim to be a psychologist or have a deep understanding of the human psyche, but I believe some answers can be found by understanding the underlying needs of both the abuser and the victim. For many abusers, there's a deep need to control relationships and the people in them. Abusive individuals who I know first-hand were abused as children. They learned how to behave from their abuser and were completely under their abuser's control when they were young. So, when they become adults, not only have they been taught how to be abusive, but they also must maintain control so they are protected from further abuse.

While these patterns are understandable, they don't justify abusive behavior. No behavior experienced by a child permits that child to become equally abusive. Everyone makes their choices. You can choose to do good, honorable, decent, kind, gentle, benevolent, and respectable things. You can also choose to be a horrible person, but it's so much more pleasant to be nice. As my dad used to say, "Niceness is nice, but meanness is mean."

The Underlying Needs

Nobody enters a relationship thinking they'll be abused. We all go into relationships with high hopes, undying love for our partner, and the expectation that our partner has similar feelings to our own. We believe, rightly or wrongly, that our partner will treat us well because they say they love us, and we believe it. We know how we treat people we love, and we expect that if our partner loves us, they'll treat us similarly.

Marriage seminars deal with these expectations. And when both partners are sincere in their faith and love for each other and need help with *how* they handle their words and actions, marriage seminars work. There are plenty of testimonials of how marriage seminars have changed lives.

An abusive partner looks for ways to further oppress the victim.

Abusive relationships are different. Marriage seminars are not helpful for those in abusive relationships because they operate on the assumption that those who attend the seminar are rational, reasonable, and want to improve their marriage. These assumptions aren't true for an abusive partner. An abusive partner looks for ways to further oppress the victim. Any Scripture verses or counsel to the victim will be used by the abuser to further oppress. Any verses or counsel directed toward the abuser are ignored or dismissed.

As victims become aware of their abuse, the abuse will escalate, so the abuser can control the situation. The more the victim learns and grows and begins to recognize how bad the situation is, the more desperate the abuser will become to maintain control of the relationship. This is why strategy and safety plans are so important.

The Abuser's Abuse

Again, abusers often grew up in abusive homes. You may notice this when you meet your abusive spouse's parents. Or they may be very good at hiding, minimizing, or dismissing any talk of abuse. However, a child's abuse and/or neglect, especially in formative years, can result in significant emotional and psychological scars that will later express in abusive patterns, including domestic violence.

On their website at https://violence.chop.edu/domestic-violence-and-child-abuse, The Children's Hospital of Philadelphia has much to say in the article "The Consequences of Family Violence":

> Domestic Violence and child abuse are truly "family violence" exposures that create and maintain a vicious cycle. . . Research shows that boys who witness domestic violence are twice as likely to abuse their own partners and children when they become adults. . . Children who have experienced abuse are nine times more likely to become involved in criminal activities. . . Child abuse victims were more likely to perpetrate youth violence (up 6.6 percent for females and 11.9

percent for males) and young adult IPV (up to 10.4 percent for females and 17.2 percent for males). Family violence . . . is one of the most direct and potentially harmful forms of violence exposure that children experience . . . not a sudden, isolated incident, but rather may involve years of emotional, psychological, and physical trauma that can escalate over time. A child can be an indirect victim of IPV as a witness and still face the serious consequences of the abuse.

The Role of Drugs and Alcohol

I have no experience with drugs and alcohol, and my abuser never used either one. But from a common-sense perspective, it's obvious that when drugs or alcohol are involved, everything escalates. Both substances reduce or eliminate normal social inhibitions, so general rules of conduct that would normally guide behavior are minimized or absent. Since abusive people already go way beyond society's general rules of conduct, substance abuse leads to further and more devastating violations of those rules.

Furthermore, a common problem facing first responders is that substance use and abuse can give users almost superhuman strength. It takes many guys to take down someone flooded with drugs. This does not bode well for the victim. If it was hard to escape from the abuser before, it would be significantly more dangerous when they're under the influence.

Substance use and abuse also change the user's mental state. Some get emotional, some get very aggressive, and the ability to be rational or respond rationally is greatly diminished. These are all bad signs for a victim. If your abuser is also a drug or alcohol user, the stakes for you are extremely high. You must escape the situation before you and your children are harmed or killed.

What Happens When You Try to Leave

Research has clearly shown the most dangerous time for a victim is when they decide to leave the relationship. I believe a big part of that is the loss of control the abuser feels. I've also read that the "If I can't have her/him, nobody can have her/him" thought is common. If the abuser is under the influence, there could be any number of reasons why danger escalates during this time, which wouldn't make any sense to a normal, rational person. To my way of thinking, it doesn't matter. It either gets really bad really quickly, or it gets really bad over a long period. It is like taking off a Band-Aid; you either rip it off quickly and experience that immediate pain or go super slowly and live in agony and dread. There's no win. There's only a choice regarding how you want to live. I can tell you emphatically that living free of the abuse is worth all the work and time it takes to safely escape your abuser.

You must escape the abuse. This can mean various things and be accomplished in many ways, but for your sake—and the sake of the children and grandchildren yet to come—you must escape. To stop abusive behaviors from being transferred to the next generation, they must be stopped now. As victims, we must not allow the abuse to continue. We need to teach our children and ourselves how to have healthy relationships without abuse.

You must escape the abuse.

The most subtle but profound change you can make is to change yourself. Study yourself and your abuser. Learn how you interact with each other, what your abuser expects you to do or not do, what your abuser is trying to accomplish with their treatment of you, how you typically react, and how they typically react. When you change how you respond, you change the dynamic. You aren't leaving or running away. You aren't accepting defeat or victory. You aren't attacking or being highly emotional. You are simply changing how you respond in a non-emotional way. This is the least threatening, least confrontational way to begin the process while determining a safe exit plan.

What Makes an Abuser Behave Themselves

In my situation, maintaining the respect of others outside the relationship was the strongest component that altered my abuser's behavior. He needed everybody to think highly of him. Having a mediator in every communication between us was, and is, the key to managing his behavior. He was forced to choose between being abusive to me and keeping the respect of the mediator.

There was a time when we had to fill out a certain legal document. My husband had the paper and went over it with the mediator and me.

"Is this everything?" I asked. "Is there anything else that needs to go on here?"

"Yes," My husband said. "That's everything."

"So, it's complete?" asked the mediator.

My husband nodded. There was some language I was uncertain about, so the mediator asked my husband to give us some privacy while we discussed it. Afterward, I signed the paper, and the mediator asked my husband to return.

When my husband sat down, he looked at the paper and said, "This section isn't filled in, so I'll just write in . . ." He bent over the paper with a pen in hand to start writing. The mediator reached over and grabbed the paper back from my husband.

"Why did you tell us this was complete when you knew it wasn't? You aren't going to change the document after it's already been signed," the mediator declared rather forcefully.

My husband said, "Well, I didn't know you would sign it."

"Right," I said, upset. "You bring a document with the express purpose of having me sign. You tell me it's all correct and ready to go; then, when I sign it, suddenly it's not complete?"

"We need to complete it with the wording we all approve," our mediator said, and we spent the next half hour hammering out language.

We were fortunate my husband made that mistake in our presence. That's when I learned I couldn't trust him to handle a document after signing it. I must be the one to mail it or turn it in, not him. If the mediator hadn't been present, I would have signed the document, and my husband would have altered it as he saw fit. And I would have been cheated.

After realizing he couldn't get away with that behavior, he didn't try it again. The horror of being caught by someone else is too much for him. If someone else from outside the family—someone whom he respects and wants to respect him—calls him out, he modifies his behavior.

NOTE TO THE UNMARRIED: Watch how your partner treats his mother and siblings. If he's mean or insensitive, talks poorly about them to you, or treats them in an abusive way, that's how he'll treat you—and much worse. Abusers always treat people better in public than they do in private, and they always treat strangers better than they treat their families.

Abusers are complex individuals who have their own needs and character traits. In part, the victim's response to these things allows the abuse to flourish. Abusers aren't mindless brutes; they behave according to their underlying needs and the traits that developed years before they met their victim. Understanding some of the issues behind the abuse can help you decide how best to go forward. Knowledge is power.

4

The Victim's Situation

Knowledge is power. We all have traits that have been developed since our earliest childhoods that make us who we are, and these are the very things our abusers exploit to their advantage and our detriment. Once we understand what they are, we can begin to get clarity and take back what is rightfully ours.

Underlying Needs of the Victim

The victim's needs are entirely different from what the abuser needs. Sometimes, a victim grew up in an abusive situation, and instead of becoming an abuser, she learned that her role was to be abused. When she grows up, she's attracted to abusers. It's what feels familiar.

These victims need help in understanding that they have value and worth. Their role is not to be abused but to be loved, supported, encouraged, and respected. They have just as much right to be happy, healthy, and loved as anyone else. They need to understand their worth.

Sometimes, because the victim knows about the abuser's past, she has compassion and empathy toward him. She believes she can provide him with the safety and love he craves, allowing him to heal from his past. Unfortunately, these victims assume their abuser is a normal, rational individual who responds to healthy environments and relationships. Instead, the abuser will never be happy or satisfied with what the victim offers. It will never be good enough. The security and love the victim offers will be rejected, ridiculed, and criticized. Each time she tries to offer more or do better at loving and caring for the abuser's needs, he considers it a pathetic attempt by someone he despises. The abuser isn't grateful or receptive to her efforts. The more she tries, the more he despises her.

Sometimes a victim grew up in an abusive situation, and instead of becoming an abuser, she learned that her role was to be abused.

In many cases, she needs to know that she's loved, and the "honeymoon" phase of the domestic violence cycle shown in the last chapter fulfills that need. Her craving for love is met during the honeymoon phases, giving her the will to hang on through the abusive phases until the next honeymoon phase comes around. Unfortunately, she doesn't realize she's believing a lie and that there's no love there.

I should interject here that many times the relationship—or lack thereof—that young girls have with their fathers is significant. When girls are rejected by their fathers, the love relationship is contaminated by abuse, or they see their mothers being abused—and their mothers cling to the belief that the abuser loves them—girls can and do become desperate for the love of a male. Many women I've known who've suffered from abuse echo the sentiment, "If he tells you he loves you, there's nothing you won't do for him." The desperation to hear those words of love and our desperation to believe them—despite any evidence to the contrary—results in all manner of undesirable outcomes: promiscuity, teen pregnancy, fatherless homes, new dysfunctional and abusive relationships, a willingness to endure abuses beyond all reason—even to the point of death—because she wants to believe that when he says those magic words, he means it.

Victim Participation

The mind is a complicated thing. As a victim, it's not like we go on a first date, the guy slaps us around a bit, and we just love it so much we decide to marry him. It doesn't happen that way. We fall in love with a façade. But what makes us susceptible to predation by an abusive person in the first place?

That's a hard question, and I probably haven't had enough counseling to formulate a comprehensive answer. But I can identify a few things in myself that may be helpful to you: an eagerness to please; a deep desire for companionship and love; quick to forgive and forget; highly empathetic; prioritizing others and relationships over myself. In short, I *really, really* want other people to be happy—specifically happy with me—and I base my worth and value on how happy (or not) my partner is with me.

> *As a victim, it's not like we go on a first date, the guy slaps us around a bit, and we just love it so much we decide to marry him.*

This type of thinking, while it may make me a "good Christian," does nothing to set boundaries or enforce them. It does not illustrate that my value and worth come from God. He created me to accomplish specific purposes that He determined for me from the beginning of time.

Instead, this thinking makes me dependent on my partner's happiness. I must sense his feelings and adjust what I'm doing, saying, or thinking to please him. If he's unhappy, it's somehow my fault, and I need to rectify the situation.

I was a ready-made abuse victim. If my husband didn't like something, I apologized. I did what I was told because I wanted him to love me. When he said his skin was sensitive and he could only use a particular kind of soap, that's all I bought. Not because he forced me to, but because I thought that would make him happy with me. Several years later, when we put the kids to bed, he said, "I want all of you to get your own soap." He was starting to hoard it. He explained, "The company might go out of business, and my skin is really sensitive, so I need it. You all get your own soap and stop using mine." Years later, we found that soap stashed in numerous hidden places after he moved out.

I regularly accepted his blame and projection. I wanted to understand how *he* felt and how *I* could do better. I often knew when I was being manipulated, but I let him do it anyway because I understood what he wanted. I wanted to make him happy with me. Of course, he could have just told me what he wanted, but he liked to manipulate me, and I thought the important thing was for me to understand what he wanted. I didn't know the importance of boundaries and enforcing them. I didn't understand that my worth wasn't linked to my husband's happiness. I didn't know that forgiving his manipulation and lies wouldn't lead to repentance and trust but would worsen everything. What I thought was being nice was an invitation for abuse.

The Bible says, "Do unto others as you would have them do unto you," and, "It's your kindness that leads us to repentance." We're taught that if we're nice, others will be nice in return. That's not true. That's not what the Bible says; our teachers have *implied* that meaning from what the Bible says. There's a big difference. And I had no idea.

The Victim's Role

Abuse doesn't reveal itself immediately because the abuser is learning about the victim. They push and test and ask questions and try things to figure out how you work. Victims tend to think the best, believe the best, and hope for the best. Victims like to give second and third chances. Victims give the benefit of the doubt. They like to trust. They think they can help, support, and encourage their abuser better than anyone else. Sometimes, victims are drawn to needy individuals who they perceive to just need "wind beneath their wings," when, actually, that neediness is a latent mental illness.

These traits are what the potential abuser needs. It's the role they need you to play. They need you to be predictable and true to your standard way of behaving. They need you to play your role consistently. Once they understand you and your way of behaving, they can do what they want to you. They can push your boundaries and trample your feelings. They can have affairs and lie; they can manipulate and deceive, all because they know how you will respond. And they know how they need to respond to your response, so you keep taking what they dish out. This is your role. Your contribution to the success of your abuser. They're counting on you to do this consistently and reliably. And that's what you do—that is until you stop.

The starting point to change is to know yourself as well as your abuser does. You need to understand how your abuser uses your predictable behaviors against you and know your predictable behaviors for yourself. And then you need to change it up. Instead of trusting, ask a lot of questions. Instead

Sometimes victims are drawn to needy individuals who they perceive to just need "wind beneath their wings," when, actually, that neediness is latent mental illness.

of giving second, third, fourth, and fifth chances, it's one strike, and you're out. You need to know yourself and change your predictable responses.

I tell you this with a strong warning: You must also know how you're at great risk when you start changing things up. You must have a strategy and plan to keep you and your children safe. Strategy and safety planning are discussed in detail in Part 5 of this book.

Enabling

What does it mean to enable? Let's say there's a family where the children are outrageously obese. Their pediatrician regularly talks to the parents about restricting food intake and making healthy eating choices, and the parents insist that they only provide healthy food in reasonable quantities. But they shop for food every other day and bring home tons of ice cream, candy, soda, pizza, twinkies, and all other assorted junk food. The children don't have established mealtime routines but constantly snack between meals and take generous portions multiple times at each meal. It's easy to see why the children are so overweight—the parents are *enabling* their poor eating habits. The parents aren't only allowing their children to become obese but encouraging it through their actions.

> *I know I didn't cause my abuse. However, I did enable it.*

Please understand that I'm *not* suggesting that victims cause their abuse. No, no, no, no, no! I'm a survivor, too, and I know I didn't cause my abuse. However, I did enable it. That's a bitter pill to swallow, but it's the truth. As a Christian, I did what Christians are taught to do: love, forgive, yield, honor, pray for, endure, believe, hope, etc. But instead of it building up our marriage relationship, those things enabled my abuser to keep abusing me.

Yes, the teachings of Christ in an abusive home enable the abuse to continue and even escalate. Why? Christ's teachings aren't correctly applied in domestic violence cases. Pastors and pastoral staff at churches often come down hard on an abuse victim, accusing her of not following Christ's instructions for wives to submit to their husbands; therefore, she's bringing the abuse upon herself. She then pressures herself and feels like she's doing exactly that—bringing it on herself by (insert whatever excuse here). Everything she hears from the pulpit and church leaders lays the responsibility directly on her shoulders.

In faith, we're encouraged to examine our hearts; don't blame other people, but examine ourselves. So, that's what we do. We look for the best in our abuser and the worst in ourselves. We try to find logs in our eyes and don't look for specks in our abuser's eyes. We pray and ask for wisdom and help. We want so much to figure out what's wrong with us, so our abuser will love us again. The Church doesn't confront the abuser, which enables him to continue the abuse because instead of exposing the evil and dealing with it, church leaders shame the victim, continue the silence, and, therefore, support the abuser in his actions. If there wasn't spiritual abuse in the home before this, the Church ensures there is now. Abuse in the Church is discussed fully in Part 4 of this book.

The Bible is often misappropriated in cases of domestic abuse. Believers are not to walk in a pattern of sin, and abusing your spouse *is* a sin. However, a commonly quoted verse says, "Judge not lest you be judged." Yet Scriptures are also clear that we *are* to judge *other believers* and confront their sins. I Corinthians 5:11-12 says:

> But now I have written to you not to keep company with anyone named a brother, who is sexually immoral, or

covetous, or an idolater, or a reviler, or a drunkard, or an extortioner—not even to eat with such a person. For what have I to do with judging those also who are outside? Do you not judge those who are inside? But those who are outside God judges. Therefore "put away from yourselves the evil person."

What if you aren't a churchgoer? You are also enablers. Your compassion and empathy, willingness to forgive and give more chances, etc. are what your abuser takes advantage of and uses to harm you. Whether or not you're a Christian, your abuser uses your character against you. So, what's the answer? Stop being nice? Stop forgiving?

Yes and no. You don't stop being you—caring, loving, forgiving, kind. You *do* stop them from using your character against you. You learn to be kind but also firm. Show just as much love and care for yourself as you show for your abuser. Learn to set boundaries. Learn to enforce them. Learn to put your happiness as high on the priority scale as you put theirs. Learn to take care of yourself. Learn that you are just as important; your opinions matter just as much, and your needs are just as important as your abuser's. It has nothing to do with religion and has everything to do with self-esteem, self-respect, and loving others *as you love yourself.*

Playing Into His Hands

Playing into his hands is a different issue from enabling. It doesn't allow the abuse to continue and escalate, but it's what he expects you to do, which keeps the cycle going. For example, if he decides he isn't getting enough attention, he gives you the silent treatment. He counts on you to eventually come to him and ask what's wrong, trying to get him to talk about whatever's troubling him. But that's not enough. He needs you to decide it's your fault and take responsibility for it. So, he continues to give you the silent treatment until you say things like, "What did I do?" or "How can I make things right?" Now he unleashes all kinds of vileness upon you because you're ready to accept responsibility for what's wrong and make it right.

This is very close to enabling, but there's a subtle difference. When you understand the game, instead of playing into his hand, you can objectively look at the situation, understand the motivation, realize your usual responses to this behavior, and choose a different response. When the silent treatment begins, you can say, "Oh. I see you don't want to talk about it, so I'm just going to go (shopping or to my mother's house or a friend's house or whatever.)"

Again, strategy and safety planning are terribly important. If your abuser controls where you go and who you see—and all your other movements—saying this may land you in the emergency room. So please, talk to some domestic violence counselors, read books, research online, and develop a safe exit plan and safety strategy first. Then you can respond in these ways, remembering what you know about your abuser and minimizing risk for yourself and your family.

You can find a list of resources at the end of the book. Start there to find help near you that applies to your situation.

How To Be Safe

Every situation is different, and yet, there are similarities across the board: The most dangerous time in the relationship is when you try to get out of it; abuse does not end but escalates over time; there's rarely only one kind of abuse happening in a relationship, etc. So, what do you do to guarantee your safety when every situation, mental state, family background, and history are different, and when what works in one situation may not work in another?

If you're trying to determine if you're in an abusive situation, the first step is to study yourself and your abuser. Evaluate yourself and your partner in an abstract/detached manner. The best way I found to do this was to get my emotions out of the way. An emotional, knee-jerk reaction to the latest hurtful thing is exactly what your abuser wants.

There was a specific event that allowed me to divorce myself from my emotional involvement, actually, two: First was when my husband said, "I only told you God said we were going to have more children to get you more interested in sex." And second, when we were in court, my attorney stated that I believed my husband had done some sexually abusive things to my daughters when they were young. My husband's attorney jumped on that and asked, "If that's true, why didn't she report it at the time? How does it make *her* any less guilty if she didn't report it?" I realized with sudden shock that he was right. If I don't speak up, I'm an accomplice.

Getting your emotions out of the way is critical. I've read about "hoovering," which is an abuser's ability to tug on your heartstrings and suck you back into the relationship like a vacuum cleaner. If you've emotionally separated yourself from the relationship, that won't happen. First, distance yourself emotionally from the relationship. Second, study yourself and your abuser and how you interact. What does your abuser say or do? What type of response does he want from you? What happens if you don't respond in your usual manner? What could you try that would be different but wouldn't spark a dangerous situation?

If you're dealing with physical violence, you must be especially careful. Physical violence can rapidly escalate to lethal situations. If you're strictly experiencing emotional, verbal, or spiritual abuse, you may have a little more leeway before a lethal event occurs. But you cannot trust that. As far as we can tell, there was no domestic violence before Chris Watts murdered his entire family and dropped his daughters in an oil tank.

I frequently mention the possibility of death because death *is* a very real possibility. However, it's not the inevitable end of all domestic violence relationships. Statistics show that well over 50 percent of female homicides are committed by an intimate partner. But statistics also show that domestic violence affects roughly 30 percent of all intimate relationships. So, most domestic violence relationships do not end with the victim's death. But several thousand deaths each year are a direct result of domestic violence, which leads to the conclusion that the possibility of death is real but not inevitable.

> ... several thousand deaths each year are a direct result of domestic violence, which leads to the conclusion that the possibility of death is real but not inevitable.

On the other hand, there may be many deaths *not* attributed to domestic violence that should be. For example, I believe Whitney Houston and her daughter were both victims of domestic violence. Both allegedly died of "suicide" the same way while living with the same man who stood to gain a great deal by their deaths. To my knowledge, he was never investigated, and life goes on. They're both dead, and he is very, very wealthy.

So, be sure to develop a safe exit strategy and plan.

Tools You Have at Your Disposal

The greatest tool in your arsenal is *you*. Research shows that abusers tend to choose individuals they believe to be smart, beautiful, awesome people. They do this so they can beat you down to make them feel like they're better than you. Remember that you weren't chosen because you're ugly or worthless but because you're someone who they felt, deep down, was better than they are, and they recognized your stellar qualities. Remember that about yourself. You are empathetic, sensitive, and caring. You love deeply and want to do what is good and right. You are intelligent. You are brave. You have value and worth just because of who you are.

Use that to your advantage. Read and study all you can about domestic violence, mental illness, personality disorders, and adult survivors of child abuse. Learn anything and everything that might be related to your family, your relationship with your abuser, and the abuser's situation before they met you. Make a list of all the resources available in your area and what they can offer you. Look online, in the government section of the phone book, or call local or county government offices. Add any resources they suggest to the list and contact those places. Keep a master list of everything available and keep multiple copies in more than one safe place. Again, resources are listed at the back of the book. It's a great starting point, but keep notes on everything else you find local to you and pertinent to your situation.

You have your brain. You have books to read. You have government resources available. What other tools do you have? If you can access funds, counseling for yourself and your children is an excellent tool. The more you can understand yourself and help your children understand what functional, healthy relationships look like and what constitutes dysfunctional, unhealthy relationships, the better. Having a spiritual community to support you would be an excellent tool, but there's a great risk that they won't understand abusive relationships and what the Word of God says about them. So be careful. You don't want to add more spiritual abuse to your burden.

Friends and immediate family are also potential tools, but again, abusive relationships are complicated and outside the capability of most people to deal with them appropriately. Besides that, they may not support you in what you're trying to do. Unless they have concrete training or experience with abusive relationships and what that means, their help or advice may be counterproductive. After I tried to file for divorce, I wrote to my dad to thank him for helping pay for my attorney. I thanked him for supporting me. He's a pastor, and his response was, "Don't confuse helping you as my daughter with supporting you."

It's critically important to spend time learning. Start with yourself. Remember who you were before this abusive relationship; remember your strengths and weaknesses. Think about all the things that you've ever loved to do. Think about what you stand for, what you care about, and what you're good at. Start caring for yourself again. Do the things you like, wear the clothes you love, go places you enjoy—rediscover yourself. Evaluate your relationship. How did it get here? How do you enable or play into your abuser's hands? What can you change to start breaking the cycle? How can you start setting boundaries and enforcing them safely? Knowledge is power.

5

Know Thyself

Knowledge is power, and it's time to dig deep to understand your needs and emotions, your bonding with your abuser, and your vulnerabilities. Why are you in this place? How did it happen? What is it about you that made you vulnerable to abuse? What has your abuser exploited in you? How well do you know yourself? Together, we'll look at the following as you:

- Identify what's happening
- Understand your emotions
- Retrace your trauma bonding
- Know your needs that made you vulnerable
- Recognize the needs that keep you attached

Identify What's Happening

If you've read this far, you're aware of what constitutes domestic violence and how it reveals itself in relationships. Now is a good time to examine yourself to uncover any of your own abusive behaviors. Victims often absorb some of the abusive behaviors and use them against other people, their children, or other family members. Just because you suffer under abuse doesn't mean you can't become abusive yourself. If you observe abusive traits in yourself and how you relate to others, you must stop immediately. Today. This very minute.

I clearly remember a time when I was standing at the kitchen sink. One of my children had done something that I don't remember anymore. I was grumpy about it and said something I don't remember. I remember that I heard myself and realized that I had the same tone of voice that my husband used on me. The tone that communicates, "You know, if you weren't so stupid, you'd already know this. If you weren't such an idiot, we wouldn't be having this conversation. If you weren't such a horrible person, I wouldn't have to deal with you." Not those words, but the tone. I would never say anything remotely like that to anyone—but the *tone*. The tone communicates volumes. If you're a victim, you know exactly what I mean. I stopped. And I hope to God that I've never done that again. Listen to yourself and ensure you are not falling into the same trap.

> *Just because you suffer under abuse doesn't mean you can't become abusive yourself.*

Assume for the moment that you don't behave abusively yourself. What do you see? What patterns show themselves? What types of abuse are in your home: physical, emotional, sexual, verbal, financial, and/or spiritual? What manifestations do you see? How does it come out? When does it come out? Are there any triggers you can identify? What behaviors does your abuser count on you to respond with? How are you enabling or following their lead? Are you silent? Are you an accomplice? Do your ways of dealing with the abuse allow it to continue?

Look at the other relationships in your life. Are there similar patterns? Does everybody take advantage of you? Do you have trouble setting boundaries with others? What about relationships with your family of origin? Your parents? Grandparents? Aunts and uncles and cousins? Do you see abusive relationships there as well? Is this a generational curse?

One of the elders in my church—the one who asked me if I was really a Christian after I brought up the abuse in our home—told me that everyone in his family simply idolized his grandmother. She was married to his grandfather, who was a brute. He drank. He beat her regularly. But she never said anything bad about him or his treatment of her. She just loved him anyway, and they idolized her for that. As he was telling me this, I couldn't help but think that they sure had a funny way of idolizing her, allowing her to get beaten up regularly by a man he couldn't bring himself to call his grandfather, instead referring to him as his "grandmother's husband." Why didn't anyone confront the man? Why didn't they do anything to protect her? Why didn't they have him arrested? None of that happened because they loved her so much that they just wanted her to keep getting beaten.

This man was in his eighties, meaning his grandmother was probably born in the early 1900s. At that time, women didn't work outside the home as a general rule. Their only way to survive was to be married to a man who would pay for their needs. Women generally accepted their fate. My complaint is not with her; she was doing the societally acceptable thing. My problem is with the idolizing family and all the descendants of that mindset, including us. Accepting abuse, staying silent, and saying we love the victim is not enough.

Understand Your Emotions

Love. What is it, exactly? What do you mean when you say that you love him or her? How do you feel? In the Facebook group "Overcoming Narcissistic Abuse," I've repeatedly seen group members say they cannot cut off contact. They can't cut ties or stop contacting their abuser. They can't stand being away from him. They love them or need him so much that they can't bear to be without him.

What does the word *love* mean to you? What does the word *need* mean to you? When your abuser says or does something nice, what does that mean to you? How does that make you feel? How do you express your feelings to your abuser? How do they respond to your feelings?

Many of us think of love in terms of feelings and emotions. Certainly, there are feelings and emotions, but love is more than that. Love is not merely emotions; it's also actions that operate in the best interest of the one we love. We put children to bed because they need rest. We cook for the family because they need to eat. We change diapers, do laundry, and pay bills because we love our family and want what is best for them. That's love in action.

So, what's the role of love as it relates to your abuser? Is it simply your emotions toward him? Or are your emotions getting in the way of what's best for you, what's best for your children, and what's best for your abuser? How can you demonstrate a true love through your actions and decisions for yourself, your children, and your abuser? How can you tweak these things to communicate love as action rather than emotion?

Make no mistake, I'm not referring to loving actions toward your abuser. No. I'm talking about love in action for *yourself*. Love in action for your *children*. Where are your emotions clouding your rational thought?

Here's an example: You're at home with the children. All is happy and peaceful. Abuser walks in. Immediately the atmosphere changes. Children are on edge; you are on edge. Abuser makes a snotty remark. Now, what do you do? This is the point where decisions are made. Do you feel hurt? Fear? Anger? Are you wondering how to keep the peace? Calm him down? Do you stay silent? Do you defend yourself or the children? Is your response geared toward what's best for the *abuser* instead of what's best for *you and the children*? Do your emotions dictate that the abuser feels loved while you and the children don't? Are your actions directed toward trying to show love to the abuser at the expense of you and the children?

You may want to start journaling as you deep dive into yourself to answer these questions. Evaluate how you're handling each situation. Write down your thoughts and analyze where you are emotionally and what you need to do differently. Here's an example: One night, I came upstairs to bed. As usual, I was the last one to go to bed. As I came up the stairs, one of my daughters exited the bathroom, and we chit-chatted momentarily. She went to her room, and I went to mine and climbed into bed. About ten minutes later, my husband grabbed his pillow and left the room. This was not entirely unusual. I'm an insomniac, so it always takes me at least an hour, if not hours, to go to sleep. About ten or fifteen minutes after he left, my youngest child, who was four at the time, started crying. I got up and went to his room and found him standing in a pool of pee, crying, while my husband was on his knees in front of him next to the bed.

"What are you doing in here?" I asked, surprised. My husband never cared for the children in the middle of the night. Never.

My husband said, "He was crying and crying, and I wondered why you never got up, so I got up to take care of him."

This was a complete and total lie, and it upset me terribly. I took care of my son and brought him into my room to go back to sleep. I was so upset that I started writing about it in my journal. As I wrote, I realized that the only explanation was that my husband was doing something to my son that he didn't want me to know about. What could that possibly be? I realized I may have walked in on the tail end of sexual abuse. I began shaking. I remembered other episodes when my children mysteriously needed me, particularly after Dad had laid down with them to "put them to bed." At first, I was upset because the man disturbed a happily sleeping child, then lied to me about it. But after journaling, I realized that the sexually inappropriate incidents he'd had with my girls so long ago weren't the end of things, and I was terrified, horrified, shaking with fear, guilt, regret, and panic that I'd allowed this abuse because I'd accepted his lies without digging deeper.

If that wasn't bad enough, I went to an elder at church and told him my concerns. The man mocked me. He said I was "shaken to my core about *everything*" and needed to accept my husband's explanations.

My emotions led me to discover a terrible truth that horrified me but had to be addressed. If you're concerned about something similar and need help figuring out if there's a reason to be concerned, start by writing. As objectively as you can, write down the incidents that concern you. Facts—what happened, when, in what order, exactly what people said. Then analyze it by looking at who benefitted in the situation and who was potentially being hurt. Dig deeper. Who gave whom what benefits, and who gave whom what bad things? Think about the looks, tone, emotions, insinuations, as well as overt words or actions. Who is benefitting? What can you change so that you and your children are on the receiving end of benefits rather than bad things? How can you handle things differently? Think, and the next time there's an episode, try to divorce your emotions from the situation so you can handle things differently.

When your abuser comes against you with something, and you're taken off guard, respond by saying that you need to think about what they said or did, and you'll get back to them. Then journal about the incident and get your thoughts down rationally. If you want to vent emotions in your journal, go ahead, but at some point, you need to let your rational mind take over and think about what is best for you, the children, and the abuser. When multiple people are involved, what's best does not necessarily mean everyone will be happy with the outcome. So rational thought processes need to be at the forefront.

Retrace Your Trauma Bonding

Trauma bonding is complicated. It happens when two or more people experience a traumatic event together. They then have a common bond that no one else shares—something serious, possibly life-threatening, that they survived together. Survivors of 9/11 are a great example, or survivors of plane crashes, sinking ships, or other similar events.

You and your abuser are trauma bonded because of what you've experienced together. It doesn't matter that your abuser was the source of the trauma. What matters is that the two of you have shared experiences that involve no one else.

My husband and I were alone in the bedroom when he shook his finger at me in utter rage and swore he'd beat the shit out of me if I ever did that again. "That" was tossing the covers back as I got out of bed to rock the baby to sleep for the umpteenth time that night. It was him and me alone after sex when he looked at me like he was possessed and acted like he was going to strangle me. I was terrified and slowly crept backward out of the room, never taking my eyes off him, trying to figure out how to grab the baby, get into the car stark naked, and lock it before he caught me. Then suddenly, he was normal again and asked what I was doing.

"You had a horrible look on your face," I said. "I was afraid."

"It was weird," he answered. "I looked at you, and you looked like a monster. You looked like my mother, with jagged teeth."

This response didn't assuage my fears. These are the types of incidents that foster trauma bonding between you and your abuser.

As you can imagine, if you and I were going down the stairs in the twin towers in New York and the building collapsed around us, yet we miraculously survived and found each other again at a nearby hospital, the emotions would be almost overwhelming. Any time you saw me again, those emotions would come rushing back, that unbreakable bond of traumatic experience you'd feel in your very soul. And no matter the time or space that separated us, when we saw each other again, those feelings of a special bond would still be as strong as ever.

This is what's happening with your abuser. A bond grows with each event, creating an emotional connection that's difficult to cut. Once again, being able to divorce the emotions from the relationship will help you. Journaling will help, counseling will help, and thinking through things rationally will help.

My husband's lawyer said that since I hadn't reported my husband's behavior, I was an accomplice, which demonstrates the strength of trauma bonding and emotional blindness. If I'd seen a stranger doing what my husband had done, I wouldn't have accepted that he was "just washing them." I

> A bond grows with each event, creating an emotional connection that's difficult to cut.

would have immediately called the police to report child molestation. But I didn't. I just told my husband not to give the girls baths anymore. And he was very angry about that.

Know Your Needs That Make You Vulnerable

You're in this relationship because certain things about your abuser fulfilled your needs. What are those things? What did he say or do? I encourage you to think deeply. Maybe he listened to you, complimented you, or made you feel special. But I encourage you to think deeper than that. Did you need him to listen because you felt that no one in your life ever had? Was your abuser the first person who made you feel like what you said mattered, that *you* mattered?

If that's the case, you probably needed to feel like you had worth. Does this make sense? Keep asking yourself why his words and actions attracted you and go deeper. See if you can come up with a few different needs your abuser met. When you discover the needs that made you vulnerable to this relationship, you can begin to counter those needs with healthy ways to get them satisfied. Being abused isn't going to satisfy any needs. Your needs are legitimate, and they need to be met. But they need to be met in a healthy way, not by an abusive relationship.

In my situation, I needed to feel like I was making a difference, contributing, and doing something worthwhile. I knew my husband grew up in an abusive home. I knew he suffered from anxiety, panic, and depression. Supporting him, encouraging him, and helping him was something I really wanted to do. I wanted him to be healthy and happy. Now, I know that no amount of support or encouragement, love, respect, help, or stability can stop someone who wants to be abusive. I can't make him happy. I can't help or encourage him when he doesn't want it.

So instead of supporting, encouraging, and helping him, I'm now doing that for my children. And I'm trying to do that for victims stuck where I was for so long. If you're reading this book, I'm getting my need met if you are supported, encouraged, and helped by my contribution. I've also learned how to release that need when someone cannot or will not accept me or what I can offer.

Your needs are legitimate, and they need to be met. But they need to be met in a healthy way, not by an abusive relationship.

Recognize Your Needs That Keep You Attached

Perhaps you feel that you cannot leave the relationship. Now is the time to examine why you feel that way. For me and every abused wife I know, finances are the biggest reason. Most of the abuse victims I know are stay-at-home moms. A few have jobs, but their money is not their own. Finances are huge. Statistics show that 50 percent of homeless women and children are homeless because of domestic violence. This is why I encourage you to start your own bank account and find any paying job you can way ahead of your planned exit time. Then you'll have some funding and employment—hopefully with benefits—so the financial needs will be somewhat manageable, especially if you can secure governmental assistance.

Other life situations may be making you feel trapped: housing, schooling for the children, transportation needs, finding and paying for an attorney, etc. Again, develop a strategy and a plan and begin implementing it long before you plan to leave. Every day you work toward your plan is one day more prepared. Even if there's a catastrophic event and you must implement your plan sooner than you thought, you'll be more prepared and ready than you are right now. The journey of a thousand miles begins with a single step. One step at a time. Take a step today.

You may also have psychological issues that keep you attached to your abuser. Maybe you need to believe that everything's fine. There's absolutely nothing wrong, and everything's good. You may need to believe that your abuser needs you. You may need to believe you aren't living in a failed marriage. You may be afraid. You may be too proud to ask for help or even admit that you need help. You may be too embarrassed or ashamed to admit or speak about what's happening at home. You may believe you deserve the treatment you're getting and are ashamed that you are so bad that you deserve it. You may be afraid that you'll get blamed or shunned by others if you talk about it. You may have already been down this road trying to get help, and it was such a bad experience that you're afraid to try again. You may need to believe that your abuser loves you, really and truly. You may believe, as many abusers say, that they'll commit suicide if you leave, and you cannot risk the guilt. You may believe that your children need their parents, and to leave their abuser would do them great harm. These beliefs, fears, needs, and doubts are real, and they keep us from doing what we need to curb the abuse, set boundaries, and strengthen ourselves for the fight to escape from it.

So, what do *you* need? You must first objectively assess if those needs are rational. Write them down and review them without getting your emotions involved. What would your counsel be if your friend came to you and started talking to you about exactly what you experienced and how you feel? When evaluating someone else's situation, we tend to be much more rational, logical, and clearheaded. So, pretend your list is not yours, but your sister's or friend's. Divorce yourself from your emotional involvement. This is so important.

Once you've identified the needs behind your feelings and actions, you can start taking different actions to get those needs met healthily rather than through an abusive relationship. Begin reading books about human needs, psychological health, setting boundaries, self-awareness, and self-actualization. Learn what you can, strategize, plan, and implement.

Ending domestic violence requires knowledge on the part of the victim. The victim must understand what domestic violence is, what motivates the abuser, and how typical responses and thought patterns enable or play into the abuser's hands. The victim needs to learn what must be changed in their own actions, thoughts, and words to disrupt the normal cycle of events. But at the same time, the victim must learn how to handle making changes safely and protect herself and her children.

> *Once you've identified the needs that are behind your feelings and actions, you can start taking different actions to get those needs met in a healthy way rather than through an abusive relationship.*

6

Help to Heal

Help to Heal Now, a nonprofit organization that I formed, is dedicated to eradicating domestic violence through a three-pronged approach:

1. Education
2. Crisis intervention and long-term transitional housing
3. Change in the legal climate

Each of these three focal points has several objectives in combatting domestic violence.

Education

Education cannot merely be a #MeToo billboard or something equally meaningless. It must be specifically targeted, address something particular, and recommend a course of action. This book is one facet of the education arm.

I also want to address domestic violence in the church. I intend for my next book to be *Pastor, What Do You Know About Domestic Violence?* It will be directed to and written for clergy and pastoral staff to give them the knowledge and tools to deal directly and compassionately with domestic violence victims and perpetrators. It will be written so that victims are helped, and perpetrators are held accountable. I want to see personal and group Bible studies for those who are victims and abusers, as well as for those who have turned a blind eye and think domestic violence is not prevalent in the church. I want a curriculum for elementary, middle school, and high school students. I want course work in college-level degree programs, specifically in the human services fields: social services, psychology, psychiatry, seminary students, nursing, medical degree programs, legal programs, law enforcement, emergency responders, etc. I want seminars at corporations and businesses to bring domestic violence out of the shadows and directly into the public spotlight. This is education—broad based and readily available.

Crisis Intervention and Long-Term Housing

The second arm is crisis intervention and long-term transitional housing. I had no idea how my husband would respond when I contemplated serving him with divorce papers. He wasn't mentally stable, and when dealing with people who aren't mentally stable, anything can happen. Do you remember the movie, *The Shining*? The release poster was of Jack Nicholson in his crazed glee, using an axe to chop through the door to get to his terrified wife. It's a classic picture of horror. It's what I feared in my home.

Imagine that you fled that scene with your children and are now in a safe house—and your two-week stay is up. Guess where you have to go? Right back to that house with that man. This is the lot of many, many DV victims. Sure, some of us have parents, siblings, or friends we can stay with, but we can only stay so long before we wear out our welcome.

Domestic violence victims need a long-term place to stay. But it must be more than that. It must be a place where we teach victims how to stand on their own two feet apart from the abusive relationship. Such shelters must entail everything from beds to sleep in, clothes to wear, medical care, job interviews, transportation, pet care, financial planning, vocational training, childcare and education, grocery shopping, rent, utilities, and everything else. My dream is to refurbish old, abandoned school buildings and transform them into living quarters and so much more. Many such buildings are enormous. I can see shops, classrooms, and security offices on the first floor, with a cafeteria and gymnasium for residents. The second (and third floors, when available) will be converted into living quarters with common bathrooms and common kitchens. The living quarters will have divided bedrooms and living spaces depending on the size of the family in residence. For the first six months, DV victims will be given everything they need and time to begin healing. This means legal help, transportation, childcare, vocational training, educational classes when needed, food, clothing, schooling for the children, counseling, etc.

How will we fund all this? Several ideas come to mind: corporate donations to refurbish the schools, tax abatement from municipalities, funding from state and federal violence against women programs, urban housing, historical building funds, and any other programs that might fit. Much of what fleeing families need are things that commonly fill landfills: clothing, shoes, furniture, bedding, towels, kitchenware, etc. We could have a driver and van collecting leftovers from garage and estate sales city wide, and that would provide the vast majority of what we need.

IS THIS DOMESTIC ABUSE?

Many old high schools have theatres, gymnasiums, and swimming pools. All these amenities can be rented out for events, receptions, homeschool groups, or playoff sporting events. I envision the women becoming entrepreneurs. Who would cater those receptions and events? Our women. Who would sell concessions at sporting events? Our women. Who will make the floral arrangements? Our women. Who will run the theatre, do the marketing, and make the theatre available to amateur productions? Our women. Who will handle the estate sale and garage sale pickup? Our women. Who will work with corporate sponsors, write grant proposals, and work with local government officials? Our women.

This leads to the next point. A six-month, take-care-of-everything program is not enough. Our women must leave the program with everything they need, including the confidence to be on their own. They need to be taught life skills to earn a living no matter where they are, be free of any outstanding legal issues, have a vehicle, a secure place to live independently, and have enough income to support themselves. So how is *that* going to happen?

This is what the long-term transitional housing program is for. Women will be expected to start the transition back into society beginning in month seven. The organization would employ them on a sliding scale. What do I mean by that? Let's say it costs the organization $500 a month for room and board for a family of four. Let's say "Bea" starts working on floral arranging in month seven. She's never done that before, so she is in training. She'll be paid for her time plus a commission. Over the next eighteen months, she'll be expected to pay the organization rent starting at a minimal amount that gradually increases to well above the local average for rental properties by the time the eighteen months is up. She should cover the organization's costs by the time she's been working for six months (one year in the program), hit the local average rental price by her twelve-month working time (eighteen months in the program), and strive to reach at least 30 percent over local average rental price by her eighteen-month working time (two full years in the program).

Just keeping the organization working and running smoothly will require a lot of people. Who will be handling the resident's pets? Someone who wants to start their own pet boarding facility. Who will be handling the laundry? Someone who will move on to be head housekeeper at a local hotel. Who will be handling security? We'll start with professionals who will then train residents who can later start their own security businesses or martial arts studios or become police officers. But in all these things, the surrounding community will help support the organization by using the services the organization offers. I know someone who would *leap* at the chance to rent a theatre for regular productions.

The final phase of the long-term transitional housing is the "Tentative Independence" phase. Since most of these abandoned schools are in the downtown area, that provides a tremendous opportunity for many other entrepreneurial adventures. First, there are many abandoned homes nearby. Some can be rented for $1 per year from the city. Some can be purchased for back taxes. All need rehabilitation. This creates more opportunities for corporate donations (and a person or team to solicit them), more opportunities for job training in demolition, salvage, construction, rehab work, plumbing, electrical work, drywall, painting, flooring, insulation, roofing, landscaping, concrete work, etc. This would also be a terrific outlet for individuals sentenced to community service; they could contribute so many hours to rebuild a house to make a home for a survivor of domestic violence.

When a house is livable again, a graduate from the program can then rent the house from the organization at 130 percent of the local average rental price. This is not to gouge the survivor.

This is to teach her to live with that level of expense, so she can comfortably move somewhere where expenses are higher than in the immediate local area. I want her to be able to find somewhere to live, whether it's in Saint Louis, Cleveland, Buffalo, Boise, Houston, Phoenix, or wherever.

She'll be on a six-month probationary independent phase. She will be completely independent of the organization but will still have access to all services and will be under the supervision of the organization. She will still have legal counsel to tie up any loose ends and financial planning, training, and budgeting tutoring to ensure she's in full command of her finances. If she needs childcare, she can hire the childcare services of the organization. If she needs to board her pet for a weekend, she may hire the pet care services of the organization, and all services will be charging standard fees for services, which will help support the organization and prepare the survivor for real-world living. After the six-month probationary period, the survivor is a full-blown graduate, complete with ceremony and certificates. She will be free to go anywhere, knowing she is fully equipped and capable of handling anything. She will also be granted access to services for the rest of her life. She may choose to stay and purchase her rental home from the organization or rent to own it, which will be handled through real estate professionals from within the organization.

The opportunities are limitless and will help women get on their own two feet—empowered, capable, healed, and ready.

Change in the Legal Climate

Changing the legal climate is a much longer-range objective because the government works at the speed of frozen molasses. There are several aspects to this vision as well. First, I have a patent pending on an app for phones. This app, called the

Data Collection System (DCS), would work as an evidence-collection device and an intermediary between the victim and emergency services. What does this mean? Let's say Bea went to court to get a restraining order. The court requires her to have documented proof that her life is in danger. What document would show that her life is in danger? Unless she has ER visits showing severe injury that came from her abuser, she has nothing.

This app can provide the proof. Using it, the victim can collect voice recordings, pictures, videos, emails, texts, social media posts, etc. But data collection is not enough. The app also disseminates the information clearly and in an organized fashion to all concerned individuals. So, when Bea goes to get her restraining order, she isn't denied; she's given the app—on a phone, if necessary. The Order of Protection will be disseminated to her abuser via all electronic means, as well as through the mail. The app connects with her case file, health care provider, attorney, and local law enforcement, among others.

Let's say Bea's abuser gets mad about the restraining order and comes to the house, demanding that she leave. She can turn on the app and record the entire event in real time. As it's recording, it's also being disseminated to all pertinent personnel in real time. She doesn't need to call the police. The app notifies the police that a violation is occurring right now in real time. They can watch the video as they're heading to the victim. In theory, they may be able to arrive before the altercation ends or escalates, and since they have the video, the abuser can be arrested for violating the restraining order. There are no delays because the process server couldn't find the abuser for three weeks to deliver the paper in person or because the victim couldn't get to the phone to call for help, wait for dispatch to answer, tell the dispatcher what's happening, wait for the dispatcher to call an available officer, and wait for the officer to finish what he's doing and head to her address. By then, the abuser is gone, and there's nothing to see. No proof. Nothing. She can make a statement, but there's no arrest because he's not there.

Furthermore, the video and subsequent police action are automatically added to her case file, sent to her social worker, sent to her attorney, and sent to her doctor so that everyone has the same information. There's no chance of documentation getting lost, misplaced, or accidentally destroyed. It's all captured. Even if the abuser figures out what she's doing, grabs the phone and breaks it, the information is still stored and available for the prosecution.

I have a patent pending on this app at the time of this writing. It's in the queue, waiting for someone to review it. I'm not a tech person, so I *really* need someone to take the vision and help develop it into its final form. I need the funding to make it happen. If it does, it could revolutionize how domestic violence cases are handled nationwide. It could be on an interconnected system, so a perpetrator in New York could be found because of a routine traffic stop in Memphis or LA. It could also be altered to fit other needs outside of domestic violence—the foster care system comes to mind. And sales of the app, nationwide, to states and municipalities, would also help to fund the organization.

Naturally, legislation would need to be proposed, changing the courts' skew to favor both the abuser and the victim equally. One of the ways I see this happening is to completely change how domestic violence cases are treated in the courts because it's not just about the law. I believe when an accusation of domestic violence is made, the accused and the accuser need to be assigned a team of three mental health professionals each: one specializing in personality disorders, one in abuse and trauma, and one in overall behavioral health. They need to meet individually with each party in the case. The findings of the three professionals should be what guides the court in its decision-making—not the attorneys, not who is more persuasive, not the court's predisposition toward innocent until proven guilty (when actually innocent is guilty until the guilty is proven guilty), not the court's predisposition that the children should be kept with an abuser.

For domestic violence to end, we have a tremendous amount of work to do. The band-aids we have now are woefully lacking, and all our organizations are hopelessly overwhelmed by the demand for their services. By not addressing the actual, deep-rooted needs of the perpetrator and the victim, we're only putting makeup on a pig and putting it back out in the pig pen. The pig needs to be bacon and the pig pen turned into a lush, productive garden. Both the perpetrators and the victims deserve to be transformed into something beneficial.

PART 3

Domestic Abuse and the Legal System

7

Problems in Our Legal System

When I filed for divorce, I asked for an order of protection. I was afraid because I didn't know what my husband would do to me and the children. The order was denied because I had no verifiable proof that my life was in danger. How exactly does one prove that one's life is in danger? Do most murderers write a note saying they intend to kill someone, then give it to them in advance so they can get an order of protection?

When it comes to domestic violence, there are many problems that relate to our legal system. My experience with the courts and domestic violence is strictly that—*my own* experience. Below are some problems I experienced when working with the legal system.

Time

Regarding the courts handling domestic violence cases, there's no such thing as time. There's no consideration of time; they get to things when they get to them and not a moment sooner. Procrastination and putting things off are ubiquitous problems detrimental to the victims. If there's one thing a victim of domestic violence does *not* have, it's time to waste. Every moment brings her and her children closer to the next violent episode, which could easily be their last.

When I filed for divorce, they needed to serve the papers to my husband in person. I was afraid of what he would do and what the children would be exposed to, so I was very specific in inquiring when—exactly—they intended to serve the papers. The process servers told me a specific time and said they knew that serving my husband papers could be dangerous for us, so they were adamant that the papers would be served at that specific time. I arranged for me and the children to sleep at someone's house, so we wouldn't be home when the papers were served. But the server didn't show up. I arranged a second, specific time. Again, they didn't show. Finally, the process server showed up completely unannounced and unplanned when we were all at home. Fortunately, my husband didn't go off the deep end physically on us then, probably because my mother was visiting, and he wanted to look good. But I had no way of knowing what he would do. The complete and total lack of regard or respect for me and my concerns about the timing was my first introduction to the complete and total incompetence of the criminal justice system regarding domestic violence.

Orders of Protection

Orders of protection, or restraining orders, are issued when the court agrees that it's dangerous for person X to be close to person Y; therefore, person X may not have contact or be within a certain distance of person Y. They're supposed to restrain person X and protect person Y. The biggest problem with that is that the order is merely a piece of paper. It's not around-the-clock security.

If person Y is out watering flowers and is talking on her phone, she may not notice that person X is at the top of the street and coming closer or is hiding in shrubbery or behind cars. Let's say she gets off the phone and sees person X on her driveway. He says he just wants to talk. He's sorry, and he just wants to set things right. He loves her and wants to make it up to her. Because you're in your rational mind and are reading this story about someone you don't know, you're probably thinking, *No! Call the police! Run inside and lock the doors!* But she's standing in her yard, talking to the man she loves, wanting to believe that he means what he says and that things will improve this time. So, she doesn't call. In doing so, she has just let her abuser know that the order means absolutely nothing and that he can do whatever he wants.

Let's say she *does* run into the house, lock the door, and call the police. The abuser walks around the house, yelling things through the window at her and banging on the doors. After a few minutes of intimidating antics, he leaves. The police show up twenty to thirty minutes later when the abuser is gone, and there's nothing to see. She can make a report if the officers are inclined, but that's it.

A woman I know had a husband who regularly came to her house to intimidate her while having an order of protection against him. He always left before the police arrived, and one day, the officer who came to the house told the woman that they were getting tired of coming to her house all the time. If she kept calling, they would stop coming.

There are numerous examples of homicide by an intimate partner that happen while under a restraining order. Sometimes, the victim even has the order on her person at the time of death.

Some studies indicate that if an order of protection is given and the abuser respects it, the victim does seem to be helped. But there are also studies that indicate that in a certain percentage of cases, the abuser considers the order a challenge, and the abuse escalates. So, there are mixed reviews on orders of protection. The best case scenario is if the abuser respects the law. Then orders of protection seem to be beneficial. However, in most cases, orders are routinely ignored by both the abusers and the legal system. And at worst, the abuser views it as a challenge to his control of the situation, and he winds up murdering people.

I have another friend who got an order of protection, and her husband routinely violated the order, stalked her, looked in their windows, and showed up at events that she and the children attended. She told me that she knew she should report him, but she felt bad about turning him into the police. After considerable urging, she began reporting violations. Because she reported multiple violations, the State took over the case and is prosecuting him, providing her with legal assistance, and shielding her from his intimidation. The case seems to be going somewhere. She no longer must pay her attorney to follow up on things because the State is handling the case on her behalf. So, in this case, not only did reporting the violations set boundaries and enforce them, but it also got the State involved in a formal prosecution against him for violating the order of protection—just wonderful! That's what is supposed to happen.

The Courts and Law Enforcement

Several problematic things seemed to be true in my case:

1. For most of the officials I dealt with, handling my case was simply their job. These people don't type on a

computer or shuffle papers at a desk; they shuffle lives through the legal system as emotionlessly and efficiently as an administrative assistant filing papers. Sometimes if a secretary doesn't feel like dealing with something, it gets set aside. That's the equivalent of a continuance or a stay. Sometimes a secretary puts things into a bin to work on later, and that's like scheduling a hearing—something that takes place a long time in the future. Then there are times when a secretary does something with the task.

2. When I appeared before the judge, it was obvious that he hadn't reviewed any of the documents or testimony I had prepared for him. He was very dismissive of me and my attorney. He wouldn't let me speak. When I could manage to talk, he said we weren't in trial, so anything I had to say would be struck from the record. Even though I was trying to divorce because of my husband's abusiveness, my husband was never on the stand. I was the one on trial. Because there were so many children involved, we were assigned a Guardian Ad Litem (a representative for the children), whose sole responsibility was to act in the children's best interests. I took the children to see him, and after meeting with the children without me being present, he said he felt that there were definite issues with their dad's behavior. He *seemed* to be aware of the things the children and I had suffered and *seemed* to be on board with protecting the children from their dad. But after he met with their father, everything changed. He talked about how there wasn't enough money to establish two different, large households to care for the children at both places. Their father should get 50 percent custody, even though the children specifically testified to his abuses toward them. Despite their testimony and mine, this

representative changed from protecting the children to protecting their father's right to be alone with them.
3. In the State of Missouri at the time, the courts mandated a certain number of hours of mediation. The Guardian Ad Litem was chosen to be the mediator. In hindsight, I feel like that put the GAL in a conflict of interest. However, that issue was not raised, and we proceeded. This proved that the GAL was nothing close to a counselor, psychologist, psychiatrist, or social worker. The GAL was not a mediator. He was not even representing the best interests of the children. To illustrate this, I need to tell a backstory:

When I first met my husband, he was fresh off a divorce from a woman he claimed had cheated on him. He told me many stories about her, which I now know not to believe. I don't know what the truth was. But what I do know is that he told me that he stalked her, and he gave examples. He told me that he would have blown her away if he'd owned a gun. I thought he was just saying stuff, like how everybody says things like, "If you take the last piece of pizza, I'm going to kill you!" Nobody really means that; it's just stuff people say.

My husband was very prone to panic attacks and was generally fearful of many things. Several times during our marriage, he'd wanted a handgun to keep at his bedside in case of an emergency. I had resisted that, in large part because of his fears. The children and I often moved about at night, and I was legitimately concerned that he would shoot one of us, thinking we were someone breaking in. He had no protection instincts for us. Early in our marriage, he asked me, "Would you mind sleeping closest to the door?"

"Sure," I replied, thinking it would be easier for me to get to the baby that way. "Why?"

"In case anybody breaks in. They'll have to go through you before they get to me!"

Fast forward to our divorce mediation. The GAL said that the purpose of mediation was to discuss important things like money, school for the children, housing options, etc. The first thing my husband wanted to talk about was getting a gun. You can imagine what instantly flashed through my mind—my husband telling me years ago that if he'd had a gun, he'd have blown away his ex-wife. And here I am, trying to become an ex-wife.

Instead of our GAL/mediator redirecting the conversation to legitimate issues to benefit the children, he looked at my husband, who said, "What father doesn't want to take his sons shooting?" To which the GAL/mediator emphatically agreed. I realized that I was dealing with a potential murder weapon. So not only was our "mediator" not mediating, but he also wasn't protecting the interests of the children when he stated his approval to put a firearm in the hands of an abusive father. Furthermore, he demonstrated that he had zero knowledge of or capability to deal with domestic violence.

4. In terms of the criminal justice system, the accused perpetrators are presumed innocent until proven guilty, and the victims, for that to happen, are presumed guilty of lying to the court until proven innocent. This is a travesty and certainly cannot be called justice. Somehow, in the courts' efforts not to unjustly imprison people, a whole host of people are treated unjustly—some, to their death.

5. The big push with the courts, in my case, was the thought, *What's best for the children?* This is such a crock. The courts don't care what's best for the children. The official position is that both parents should

have equal access to their children. I'll never believe that a child is more negatively impacted by being *without* the abuser than by being forced to *be alone* with the abuser for years. What's best for the children is that they be kept safe, that their basic needs are met, and that they're loved. Any allegations to the contrary deserve the respect of being heard and investigated. If the courts cannot or will not investigate allegations of abuse, they cannot claim to be interested in what's best for the children.

Money

In my case, the courts equated the children's well-being with money. Whichever parent had the greatest opportunity to earn the most money was the parent they wanted the children to be with. While children who grow up with more fluid money could, in theory, be better taken care of from a physical standpoint, more money doesn't guarantee that they'll be safe, have their basic needs met, or be loved. The victim is certainly not going to have control of the money. That's part of the abuse. Therefore, the basic premise of awarding custody to the parent with the most money is wrong at best, downright deadly at worst.

There are all kinds of ways for an abuser to continue his abuse. A friend of mine got an order of protection, as well as majority custody of the children. She had been a stay-at-home mom, so her husband was ordered to pay a certain monthly amount to provide for the children. He promptly quit his job so he'd have no income. He used that tactic to force his wife and children into homelessness and destitution. At the time of this writing, he still doesn't have a legitimate job and has been paying around $30 a month for child support. In fact, he's petitioned the court to have *her* pay *him* money. Abusers have no conscience.

Hearings

There are two different types of hearing. There is hearing that relates to using your ears. Sound goes in, the brain processes it, and decisions are made. The other type of hearing is more abstract and involves understanding what's being said coupled with the wisdom to apply what's said and what's left unsaid to determine a course of action based on a discernment of the truth.

I can only guess that a hearing is supposed to be when the judge "hears" the different aspects of the case at hand. There are a great many variables that come into play here:

- Time: The courts have only a set amount of time to devote to each situation. When I went for a hearing, the courtroom was filled with people—not observers, but people waiting their turn to present their case. Speed is of the essence.
- Experience: When a judge or an attorney has handled something a million times, they're much faster. They can see patterns that have appeared many times before and make decisions without having to hear everything. While this expedites cases, it also deprives individuals of their time to be heard and prevents specific grievances from being aired. It prevents details from being uncovered. It also communicates a certain level of boredom with routine cases, thus leading to hasty decisions and outcomes, which results in dismissing testimony, evidence, or the presentation of a case as unimportant or irrelevant. In domestic violence cases, these unaddressed issues could have lethal consequences.

- In my case, the judge obviously didn't put much stock in my allegations of abuse. I created dozens of pages of testimony that he never read. He cut off my answers and struck them from the record if they seemed to be heading in a direction that might look bad for my abuser. He said things to me like, "You just want more freedom than you did when you first got married, don't you?" Isn't that a leading question? Aren't legal people forbidden from leading the witness? When questions came up about finances, the judge asked my husband, "Well, it's not like you've got a boat hidden somewhere, right?" I was seeking a divorce because of *the abuses* we suffered, but I was the one who had to defend myself on the stand. My husband was never asked to testify or even answer any questions. It was a sham. And despite my second oldest daughter's testimony of abuse, the court was considering a 50 percent custody arrangement, with my second oldest daughter acting as a surrogate mom while the children were away from me. The court was about to rule that she would be forced into indentured servitude under my abusive husband for the next ten years—until my youngest child was no longer a minor. So, I dropped the case. And my husband, the narcissist that he is, viewed the court's discussions as supporting him; therefore, the abuse escalated. And I had nowhere to go, no place to escape or get relief. I needed help, but there was nothing that could help me.

Mental Illness

I firmly believe that a person cannot abuse another significantly without having a mental illness. A person does not mistreat another, especially someone they profess to love, without being mentally disturbed. A person does not continue to mistreat another, escalating to other types of maltreatment over time, and feels justified in doing it without having some kind of mental issue.

A lawyer or a judge is not in a position to make those kinds of diagnoses. They're capable of listening to evidence and seeing what is presented. In Ted Bundy's case, he was generally described as attractive and charming. He didn't look like anybody's idea of what a serial killer looked, talked, or acted like. Thankfully, the jury convicted him of his murders and put him behind bars.

> *I firmly believe that a person cannot abuse another significantly without having a mental illness.*

But when the perpetrator is an abuser, can the judge get past his appearance? He sees a calm, well-adjusted person standing in front of him who's accused of all kinds of things by someone who appears desperate. Victims tend to get emotional if things don't seem to be going how they want. Which one looks more rational, sane, and capable to the judge? You got it—the calm, charming person who denies they could ever hurt the alleged victim. They say they love the victim and would never do any of the things they're accused of. Meanwhile, the victim pleads for help, begs for mercy, and can't understand how the judge believes what the abuser says.

Can judges see past appearances to realize cause and effect? Can judges understand that emotional pleas and desperation are *the result* of the abuse? Can they see that the next step could be a funeral if they don't rule to protect the victim? Are judges even qualified to determine that a life of unending abuse for a child is better than a life protected from that abuse? Are victims' pleas to be heard and protection from their abuser so off-putting that a judge must rule in favor of the calm, charming one?

In high-profile criminal cases where the accused is calm and unemotional, that's often interpreted to mean they have no remorse. It's a strike against the accused. But in domestic violence cases, being calm and unemotional seems to work in their favor.

A recent high-profile case was the case of actors Johnny Depp and Amber Heard. Obviously, we couldn't be in the courtroom to see and hear all the evidence. For those of us who rely on the media for information, it appeared that the evidence indicated that Johnny Depp was the one who Amber Heard physically abused. The courts in Britain ruled against him, and he lost major acting contracts. Amber Heard still has her acting contracts. At this writing, Mr. Depp plans to appeal.

The US defamation trial between Amber Heard and Johnny Depp just concluded. The trial wasn't about the abuse but about an article Ms. Heard wrote, which Mr. Depp states is defamation. That's the extent of the trial: Was the article she wrote defamation? However, as evidence was submitted in the court of public opinion, it appears that Amber Heard was the aggressor in the relationship much of the time. That being said, both sides are desperately in need of good counseling. The US courts agreed that Ms. Heard's article was intentionally defamatory and fined her. Kudos to the attorneys who publicly exposed the lies, falsehoods, vindictiveness, projection, and gaslighting that permeate abusive relationships.

This further illustrates my point that the courts cannot ascertain the actual truth in a domestic violence situation because they aren't trained in psychology, social work, etc. They can only go on who is more persuasive. In my experience, the abuser is far more persuasive than the victim. How else could the abuser abuse the victim for years and years, and the victim *still* feels it's their fault or that they deserve it, or for some reason, the abuser does not need to be held accountable?

8

Solutions for Our Legal System

Our legal system moves with all the speed of a dead turtle. Since our laws are made by state and federal legislatures, we must work through the legislatures to make changes. This means finding someone willing to draft a bill, then finding enough people to support it to go to committee. Then it must make it out of committee for a vote before it goes to the other chamber, and on and on. At any time, it can be dropped—or the governor or President could veto it. It's a long and arduous process to get an issue into law, and then the question becomes how to enforce the new law.

This chapter presents ideas for consideration rather than things in place now. But productive change can happen if we all work together, contact our legislators, and lobby for change in our State and Federal governments.

Time

As I mentioned in Chapter 6, I have a patent pending on an app concept. This app could help solve the time problem in a few different ways:

1. Evidence can be collected, uploaded, and disseminated in real time. When a phone call from the perpetrator occurs, the user can record it and automatically send it to all pertinent legal and professional individuals involved with the case. The same is true for all interactions and evidence that pertain to the case. Information is immediately uploaded to permanent files that multiple professionals can access.
2. Communication between involved parties can occur electronically instead of in person. The system will keep everything organized by date and individual, court case number, etc.
3. Victims will not have to call 911, explain everything to a dispatcher, and wait for an officer to arrive. The evidence will directly go where it needs to go, alerting law enforcement if the victim needs help in person.
4. The app should expedite court hearings as well. The app will organize evidence into a history, making patterns of abuse clear and concise. Judges will not have to listen to hearsay or conflicting recollections between witnesses because the evidence will be collected in the case file for review.

Orders of Protection

What should happen if there's a violation of the order of protection? Quite simply, there must be a report *every single time*.

There must be documentation of the violation. If the abuser shows up and starts looking in the windows, then you take video or snap pictures. Use your phone or anything handy. If the abuser sends threatening texts or social media posts, take screenshots. No matter how minor, every violation must be documented and reported. This creates a history, shows a pattern, and presents evidence that can be submitted as proof of the violation.

Until the app is available, you must be painstaking in your data collection and disciplined in disseminating that information. Statistically and experientially, abuse does not get better over time. It always escalates, slowly but surely. It's so slow that for people like me who lived with it for twenty-five years, when I look back on pictures from when we were first married, I don't even recognize my husband. It's like he was a different person. The person I believed he was, the person he was faking—it was all a show, a façade.

Documentation and reports can ensure that the pattern and history will be shown to the authorities. Suppose it can be demonstrated that a variety of abuses have occurred and that the frequency and severity have escalated over time. In that case, the court should have no recourse but to rule in favor of the victim. I say *should* because there are still the variables of time, experience, and preconceived ideas that could play a role in the court's decision-making process. But your evidence will be rock solid.

Social Services

The courts need to change how they process domestic violence cases, and legislators should consider how they might change the laws to expedite the process, which would be required for what I propose. The current system is highly inefficient and doesn't justly address domestic violence. Laws and implementation methods need to be changed. Instead of a judge having the power to make decisions without a professional assessment of the parties, a panel of three social professionals should be used; one specializing in trauma and abuse, including, but not limited to domestic violence; one specializing in behavioral health; and one specializing in personality disorders. Involving these three professionals should be court ordered to evaluate both parties for three to six months or until a consensus on a diagnosis can be reached. Once the panel has reached a consensus, they may advise the court regarding a course of action that is just for all parties concerned.

The current system is highly inefficient and doesn't justly address domestic violence.

This will solve several problems. First, it will solve the problem of judges and attorneys being placed in the position to discern the character of the alleged victim and alleged abuser. Especially without the evidence from the app, the courts simply rely on the impressions the victims and abusers make and the persuasiveness of the legal counsel for each. Given the psychology of what is happening at home and in the courtroom, this puts the victims at a terrible disadvantage. To make a judgment, the judge needs an unbiased and impartial conclusion drawn from a panel of experts rather than relying on impressions and persuasion.

While this will undoubtedly require the social professionals' time, the overall time for the case will be reduced because the court can make a final decision once the professional assessments have been filed. There will be no need for stays, continuances, or other hearings. The final decision can be made as soon as the three professionals file their reports. Assuming both parties are committed to their original stated positions, it will take at most six months for the courts to go from the first contact to the final decision. Six months of meeting with both parties for evaluation meetings should be adequate time for the professionals to reach a consensus. The consensus could be reached much sooner if one party refuses to attend the evaluation meetings or if the evidence collected by the app is overwhelming.

The biggest barrier to establishing a panel of experts is the expense of hiring the professionals required to evaluate the number of domestic violence cases. However, according to the Educational Fund to Stop Gun Violence, between 2003 and 2014, 10,018 women in the United States were victims of homicide. If we use our statistic of 58 percent resulting from domestic violence, that's roughly 5,810 women. Averaging that number over eleven years, that's roughly 528 women each year who were murdered by their intimate partner.

In recent years, the incidence of female homicide has grown from roughly three women per day to almost four women per day. There doesn't seem to be a consensus about how many are related to domestic violence, but the question is, are these lives worth investing in mental health evaluations? Are the children involved worth the mental health evaluations? Will the benefits over the long term offset the costs in the short term? These are questions that need to be answered. These are research projects that need to be studied.

> *In more recent years, the incidence of female homicide has grown from roughly three women per day to almost four women per day.*

If professional evaluations result in saving women's lives, can we deduce that their escape from domestic violence will result in better productivity, health, and child-rearing? Will better child-rearing result in fewer mental health issues for the next generation? Will protecting the victim and the children from further abuse help break the cycle of domestic violence, thus reducing the incidence of these issues five years from now? Ten years from now? Twenty years from now?

What if, instead of providing court-appointed attorneys for those who cannot afford to pay, the court appointed mental health professionals in domestic violence cases? This would reduce the attorneys' hours, cost the court about the same amount for three mental health professionals as it would for one attorney, and resolve domestic violence cases in six months instead of the years it takes now. My guess is it would save the court system a ton of money to use this protocol instead of attorneys and family court. For people who can afford to pay an attorney, it will probably cost the same or even less to use three mental health professionals instead of attorneys, and it will take six months at most.

Crisis Intervention and Long-Term Transitional Housing

Here's why crisis intervention and long-term transitional housing must be a huge priority for any program that addresses domestic violence: Survivors need a place to go where all their needs are taken care of, and they can solely focus on healing. Programs must be developed in which survivors go from being desperate victims to overcomers with a job, a place to live, an understanding of budgeting and healthy habits, and a firm understanding of how she and her children can make it successfully without being involved in a destructive and dangerous relationship. Currently, most shelters can take a victim for two weeks at most. Before I served my husband with divorce papers, I tried to find a shelter for my children and me. I called several places—no room. Nothing. There was no room for someone who had seven children.

It's my position that while crisis intervention and short-term crisis housing are critically important, the major flaw in these shelters is that time spent there is necessarily limited. For many women, they have no option but to go back to the abusive relationship. It's not wise to leave an abusive relationship for a few days and then return home. Abuse can escalate in these situations.

> *... survivors need a place to go where all their needs are taken care of and where they can solely focus on healing.*

Long-term solutions are desperately needed, as I described in Chapter 6. It's necessary to immediately remove victims from a situation when a critical event is happening. But it's even more necessary to give victims the tools they need to leave the abusive relationship behind and successfully stand on their own two feet. This requires counseling, coaching, teaching, training, and time invested in their lives. They must start where they are and take baby steps as they're ready, to get them from where they are to complete and secure independence. When done right, the program could pay for itself and would be a tremendous help for victims both now and as the children grow up in a safe and secure environment.

Legislative Changes

Since the purpose of our judicial branch of government is to interpret the law to make changes in the laws that make sense and protect victims of domestic violence, the legislative branch needs to get involved. This is undoubtedly a long, drawn-out process. Many individuals, legislators, and organizations are trying to make changes to the laws. I've suggested some ideas in earlier chapters and have applied for grants for both the app and the long-term transitional housing. I've also spoken to an

Assistant Attorney General of the State of Missouri during her time in office. But I need collaborators. I need funders. I need other supporting organizations willing to come alongside me. Maybe somebody reading this book can help! Much more needs to be done. Legislators must be written, called, and visited. Legislation must be written, discussed, voted upon, passed, and signed into law. Then and only then can the legal climate change.

Of course, lawyers know the law, but they don't necessarily know what's best for the victims, families, or perpetrators. Winning in court is not necessarily winning for justice. The laws passed must help lawyers and judges focus on justice, not winning and losing, but on *justice*, including safety and security for the victims and appropriate penalties for abusers. A balance of legislation designed to protect victims and hold abusers accountable for their actions, along with the prompt enforcement of the laws and the involvement of the social sciences to address mental illness and the motivations behind abuse will begin to curb domestic violence among the adult population.

A great misapplication of justice pertains to the difference between sentencing perpetrators who kill their victims vs. victims who kill their abusers. The Michigan Women's Justice and Clemency Project, through the University of Michigan, has published information and recommendations regarding the legal handling of domestic violence cases. It cites that when women are murdered by their intimate partners, the perpetrator averages a sentence of about ten years. But if a woman murders an abuser, she's more likely to be given a life sentence.[2]

Much work needs to be done to bring justice to domestic violence victims. The psychological and behavioral issues

---

[2] Michigan Women's Justice & Clemency Project Position Statement, 2018, http://websites.umich.edu/~clemency/position.

behind the violence and the traps that keep victims in these relationships must be identified, addressed, dismantled, confronted, and dealt with appropriately. My solutions are the Data Collection app, using a panel of three mental health professionals to aid in the judicial process, and long-term transitional programs designed to help victims learn how to succeed and thrive apart from the abusive relationship.

PART 4

Domestic Abuse and the Church

9

What Does God Say About Domestic Violence?

Anyone who considers themselves a believer or religious might say that they want to live a life that's in accordance with God's Word. They want to do what is right. Abusers say the same thing to trick everyone into thinking they're a Christian or hold traditional religious values. Victims often look to their religion for answers about how to handle their situation. They counsel with their priest, pastor, elder, or teacher to try to figure out how they're supposed to behave in such a situation. The problem is that much of the advice given—even the verses found in Scripture—is taken from a discourse dealing with a healthy set of circumstances, not domestic violence. Thus, the scriptures are misinterpreted, and the advice given

> *The problem is that much of the advice given—even the verses found in Scripture— are taken from a discourse dealing with a healthy set of circumstances, not domestic violence.*

makes everything worse.

    Church leaders cling to several key tenets, such as divorce is not an option. This is a foundational principle all over Christendom, and churches worldwide come down hard on the whole "God hates divorce" thing. I have had Christian people tell me that if my husband kills me, it must be God's will for me, and I must submit even unto death and teach my children the same. What? God *wills* for a woman to suffer and be murdered at the hands of a "Christian" husband? The book of Romans tells us that God can work all things together for the good of those who love God. That is entirely different from saying that God wills a God-fearing woman to be murdered by a "God-fearing" husband. The statement that God hates divorce comes from a passage in Malachi, chapter 2 (NKJ):

> 13 And this is the second thing you do:
> You cover the altar of the Lord with tears,
> With weeping and crying;
> So He does not regard the offering anymore,
> Nor receive it with goodwill from your hands.
> 14 Yet you say, "For what reason?"
> Because **the Lord has been witness**
> **Between you and the wife of your youth,**
> **With whom you have dealt treacherously;**
> Yet she is your companion
> And your wife by covenant.
> 15 But did He not make them one,
> Having a remnant of the Spirit?
> And why one?
> He seeks godly offspring.
> **Therefore take heed to your spirit,**
> **And let none deal treacherously with the wife of his youth.**
> 16 "For the Lord God of Israel says
> **That He hates divorce,**

For it covers one's garment with violence,"
Says the Lord of hosts.
"Therefore take heed to your spirit,
That you do not deal treacherously."

I want to point out the connection made between treachery toward your wife and divorce. He says, "Therefore take heed to your spirit, and let none deal treacherously with the wife of his youth. For the Lord God of Israel says that He hates divorce, for it covers one's garment with violence." Notice that there's no mention of a "certificate of divorce" as is mentioned elsewhere in Scripture. In fact, there's no mention anywhere of any formal or legal divorce proceedings or anything remotely regarding the law. It says, *let none deal treacherously, for the Lord hates divorce.*

This passage doesn't teach that divorce is not an option. Instead, the verse teaches that treachery against your wife—and I think it's safe to say against your spouse—is the act of divorce. And that is what God hates. It's not the certificate—not the legal document. It's the treachery against your spouse and, by extension, treachery against your offspring. Domestic violence is treachery against children because they'll have a tough time learning how to be honorable life partners and parents.

If there's abuse in the home, there's treachery. No doubt. This whole chapter deals with how God hates it. It makes Him sick. He isn't going to listen to those who are treacherous. He won't accept their offerings or supplications. He is sickened by it. When this is going on in the home, the victim is an especially tragic kind of widow, and the children are especially tragic fatherless ones.

Some teachers say this passage refers to the practice in ancient times when men issued

If there's abuse in the home, there's treachery. No doubt.

divorce certificates to women for no reason and abandoned them to their fate. That was certainly an issue, and that could be something this passage references. But if that were the entire issue, the passage would have been worded differently. It would have communicated that the act of divorce was the treacherous thing. Instead, God is clear that treachery *against the wife of your youth* is wrong. The treachery IS the divorce. Not the divorce is the treachery.

People who quote this passage in Malachi fervently believe that if the Bible says God hates something, we should never, ever do that thing. We can expect Bible studies on these things and sermons telling us all the evils of the things God hates, just like how churches treat divorce. Here are other things God says He hates:

God says He hates lying, dishonesty, and false oaths *nine times.* And in the Book of Revelation, John writes that all liars have a place in the lake of fire. Christian denominations specifically call out divorce as something a good Christian must never do. We all know that truthfulness is of God, and we all know that the truth sets us free, and we all know that we should tell the truth. Abusive people, Christian or not, lie like the proverbial rug about absolutely everything—*everything*.

Do pastors talk about the evils of lying as they talk about the evil of divorce? Are there Bible studies about not lying, about restoring yourself to a place of truthfulness? Do pastors include dishonesty in the sins that send you to hell along with divorce? When was the last time you heard a pastor mention lying or truthfulness in any teaching that had anything to do with daily life or interactions with others? Have you ever? I haven't. But I've heard about the evil of divorce and many insinuations about the eternal destiny of those who engage in the practice. It goes without saying that we shouldn't lie; therefore, nobody talks about it, and we all carry on like everyone always and only speaks the truth. Not only is this completely dishonest, but it also implies to the victim living with an abusive liar that for the abuser to be the Christian they say they are, they must be telling the truth. And since we are to believe all things, and they're telling the truth, we need to believe our abuser. And *that*, my friends, is a lie, which God says He hates nine times.

Shortly after dropping my divorce case, I watched *A Bug's Life,* the Disney movie about ants being enslaved by wicked grasshoppers. There's a scene when the director of the flea circus finds the troop of bugs that are planning to save the ants from the grasshoppers. He's all excited to find them because their show (which they thought was a total disaster) was a big hit, and he wanted them to return to work for the circus and perform this act. This is where the ants discover that instead of being the hero warriors they thought they were, the bugs are circus performers.

The ant colony is devastated by the trickery and betrayal of the ant, Flick, who was responsible for finding the warrior hero/circus bugs. He lied to them, and the whole colony of ants was devastated by the betrayal, and they banished him from the colony. I remember thinking to myself that it was nothing. I'd been lied to for years about everything under the sun, yet I couldn't file for divorce without being considered a backslidden Christian. I couldn't *not* believe the lies because my "Christian" husband said he was telling the truth. I had to believe him because "Love always trusts." They said I was in sin for not following the Scriptures if I didn't believe him. If I did believe him, I was also in sin for not discerning whether the spirits were of God.

Let's look at Ananias and Sapphira, who agreed to sell a piece of land and bring a portion of the sales price to the disciples. Acts Chapter 5:1-10 tells the story. They sold the land for X dollars. But they wanted to keep a portion of the sale price for themselves. The Apostles, being the discerners that they were, decided to test this couple's truthfulness. Ananias brought Y amount to Peter. Peter was not stupid. He knew that a one-bedroom mud house in Judea with so much land was worth roughly X amount. But Ananias brought Y. So the question was, did Ananias get a bad price for his property? Or was he positioning himself to appear like others who brought the entire price of what they'd sold? Did he keep some back for himself, and if so, why?

So, Peter asked him, "Is this the whole price?" And Ananias revealed his heart. He lied. He said, "Yes, it is." He didn't have to do that. He could have told the truth. But he wanted to look good. He didn't want Peter to think he kept something for himself. He thought he could look good *and* have some extra cash. Next thing he knows, he's standing before the judgement seat of God Almighty, trying to explain why he lied to the Holy Spirit.

This is an excellent example of how God deals with someone who lies to Him. Can we agree that lying is contrary to the nature of God as revealed to us in His Word?

God says He hates wickedness, evil, etc., twelve times. The question, then, is, "What is wickedness, evil, etc.?" Would triangulation be wicked—the pitting of two people against each other to benefit the one causing the strife? What about saying hurtful or cruel things? What about physically injuring or neglecting someone? What about making someone feel like they're losing their mind, going crazy, or causing them to commit suicide? What about self-protection to the point of sacrificing the health or safety of another? What about threatening, blackmailing, or sabotaging another? What about rage heaped upon another? What about manipulating someone? What about destroying someone's self-respect, self-worth, and confidence? What about constantly criticizing another, putting them down, or humiliating them?

Abusive people do all these things and more, all day long, every day. Every single day. These aren't aberrant behaviors. These are natural, consistent, ubiquitous behaviors of an abuser. God says he hates wickedness and evil twelve times but only mentions divorce once.

God says He hates perversity three times. What is perversity? Most of the time, we think of sexually inappropriate behavior as perversity, things like lusting after, raping, photographing, and watching daughters, or having sexual addictions like addictions to porn. Things like sex trafficking your spouse or children. Yes, it happens. Not all abusers are that bad, of course, but some are. And many, many victims I've talked to about domestic violence have reported sexual addictions in their abusive partners. God mentions perversity three times but divorce only once.

God says He hates the proud four times. How does pride enter here? It's interesting. Many abusers think of themselves as being so smart, cunning, and charming that they can get away with practically anything. Nobody believes the abused person, and everyone believes the abuser. At the same time, abusive people are known to choose victims who they believe, deep down, are better than they are. So, on one hand, they have low self-worth, probably from the abuse they suffered in their formative years.

But on the other hand, they choose someone they consider excellent, so they can push them down to elevate themselves. Is that pride? I think so. It's twisted, but the result is that they elevate themselves in their minds far above the spouse they once thought was so great. They despise the victim and hold themselves up as the most important, smartest, and most deserving of respect—the mostest and the bestest. Isn't that what pride is? Having too high of an opinion of yourself, with the result being that you think more highly of yourself than anyone else? And doesn't this mean that the basic command to husbands to love their wives and the basic command to all Christians to not think more highly of themselves than they ought are being violated? God speaks of hating the proud four times but of divorce only once.

God says He hates monuments to other gods twice. Monuments to other gods—what could that mean? Idols? Statues of Buddha? Could it be other things, too, like fine clothes, cars, or status symbols designed to impress others? Maybe even parading the victim around in hot, sexy clothes to make the abuser look like he's really something to have such a fine specimen for his wife. God includes another thing He says he hates in Scripture: the palaces of the wicked. I would submit these are the fine estates of those who use their property to further the evil they do or hide it, as in the case of Jeffrey Epstein. He says he hates the palaces of the wicked once, along with refusing to hear the law (common to every "Christian" abuser); loving violence (common to every "Christian" abuser); sowing discord (common to every "Christian" abuser); shedding innocent blood (common to many "Christian" abusers); and being double-minded (again, common to every single "Christian" abuser).

Why is it that these other things, most of which are things an abusive person is or does continually, don't carry the weight that divorce does? Why is it OK for these things to occur daily in an abusive home, but divorce is absolutely prohibited? Is there something in the Scriptures I'm missing?

God hates perversity and wickedness. But if a victim is married to someone who regularly is perverse and wicked, she can't divorce that. She must stay married and submit in all things as unto the Lord, turn the other cheek, take the log out of her eye, and be without sin before she can cast the first stone. After all, Christians aren't supposed to go to court over issues with each other; issues are supposed to be handled by the church. So, what is the church doing?

The Lord specifically states in Proverbs 24:11-12, "Rescue those being led away to death; hold back those staggering toward slaughter. If you say, 'But we knew nothing about this,' does not He who weighs the heart perceive it? Does not He who guards your life know it? Will He not repay everyone according to what they have done?" What a powerful statement! This passage more than applies to domestic violence. The Lord commands that we intervene in dire situations and tells us in no uncertain terms that ignorance is no excuse.

To learn more about how God views domestic violence, we must examine several accounts of domestic violence in the Scriptures. There are five specific examples to examine, two of which deal with spouses and three of which deal with abuse within the family unit. We'll approach them chronologically: Cain murdered Abel; Abraham trafficked Sarah; Saul assaulted and attempted to murder David; Nabal was a drunken jerk to Abigail; and Amnon raped and despised his sister Tamar.

Cain and Abel

You're probably familiar with the account of Cain and Abel. Cain raised crops; Abel raised livestock. They each brought gifts for the Lord, and God was pleased with Abel's gift but not with Cain's. This made Cain angry, and he took his brother out to the field and killed him. God saw this and confronted Cain, who acted like he had no idea where Abel was and said the infamous, "Am I my brother's keeper?" God immediately banished Cain. Cain said he was afraid someone would kill him, so God put a mark on Cain, so everyone would know not to kill him.

A few takeaways from this account regarding domestic violence: The other family members weren't required, encouraged, guilt-tripped, or manipulated into giving Cain another chance.

This domestic violence situation resulted in a homicide. We know that some homicides related to domestic violence come after many threats, but other homicides happen completely without warning. We also know that if a victim feels like homicide is likely, and they get an order of protection, what does this mean? It means that they believe their life is in danger, but until they are dead, they must keep living with the possibility. If they die, then the State may or may not prosecute, and the perpetrator may or may not be convicted and may or may not serve time. It all depends. Sometimes justice is served, but sometimes not.

There must be enough evidence to tie the perpetrator to the crime. The perpetrator is considered innocent until proven guilty. Of course, God didn't need evidence because He knows all things. But in today's Christianity, victims aren't allowed the relief of having the perpetrator banished or even removed from the church. Victims are expected to forgive and show proof of that. They're lectured on the evils of bitterness. The focus of all parties must, above all else, be on the restoration of the marriage. If the victim isn't on board with that, the whole church will unite behind a wall of disapproval that puts the onus on the victim to restore the marriage and desire that restoration above all things.

Cain murdered Abel. I've heard people say the church doesn't tell murder victims to forgive. Obviously, they can't. They're dead. I know some people who went to a church that loved their pastor. Just loved him. One day, they woke up to learn that the pastor had beaten his wife so badly that she was in intensive care. They also learned this wasn't the first time. Not a soul in that church had known she was in danger. She bore her secret completely alone.

The State prosecuted the case. I never learned the outcome, but the church I was attending at the time was very critical of *the wife!* The victim should not have pressed charges, they said.

(Even though she was not the one pressing charges, the State was prosecuting the abuser.) They said that matters should be handled within the church, not in courts. Where was her heart of forgiveness toward her husband? When Jesus was nailed to the cross, He forgave. She should do the same.

Fortunately, the victim's congregation didn't share such an ungodly view. The pastor was banished, exactly as God had treated Cain. That's how all abusers should be treated. If domestic violence comes to light, the abuser should be banished from the church. A big reason for that, besides the fact that God responded to Cain this way, is that if an abuser goes to the same church as the victim, realistically, what will happen? Are they expected to sit together because that makes them look like a happy, believing, loving family—which is a lie? Do they sit apart when that makes everyone ask why they aren't sitting together?

While this would be a great opportunity for the victim to speak about what they've been experiencing at home, this kind of truth-telling could be widely viewed as gossip or slander. We don't speak of such things inside the hallowed halls of our churches, particularly when the abuser is sitting off by their lonesome, looking all forlorn and rejected, and eagerly lapping up pity and compassion from those who judge the victim to be bitter and unforgiving. This will also give many in the church a chance to chide the victim for their harsh judgement toward the perpetrator when the objective should be on the restoration of the marriage. Remember, what God hath joined together, let no man put asunder. Besides, if the objective isn't restoration, then either the victim is bitter, which is a sin and leads to hellfire, or the victim is abandoning the covenant made before God and witnesses with the abuser, and everyone knows that God hates divorce. It's a Catch-22.

Some people may think that banishing the perpetrator eliminates their opportunity to be supported among believers who are friends, people who can walk with them on the road to restoration. There are a couple of issues with this:

- They've been walking the road with you (their friends) for a while and abusing their family the entire time, and you've either had no clue or have done nothing.
- Why on earth would you want to restore an abuser to a victim when statistics prove that abusers don't stop abusing but get worse over time? If you want to walk with the abuser yourself, do so. But don't try to guilt trip a victim into staying intimately connected or living with someone who could very well murder them and their children. Righteous indignation by well-meaning but totally misguided churchgoers forces victims to endure years of abuse while putting on a fake face at church so nobody knows.

Back to Cain and Abel. No mercy or statements of forgiveness were required from anyone toward Cain. God didn't even allow Cain to apologize. Clearly, it was because Cain was unrepentant, as are nearly all abusers. Abusers will say whatever they have to say to escape consequences, and Cain is the perfect example. First, he lied and said he didn't know where Abel was. Then when God told him he'd be banished and would be a fugitive and vagabond for the rest of his life (the consequences of his actions), Cain said it was too much for him to bear (trying to guilt-trip God). Then he said that anyone who found him would kill him (pity party for the murderer). Thus, God put a mark on him so no one would kill him, and Cain left the presence of God. Never once does Cain show remorse or sorrow over his actions.

I'm suggesting that the church put its condemnation on the perpetrator instead of the victim.

God never says that anyone had to reconcile with Cain or restore the relationship. God never suggests that it's the believer's responsibility, especially family members, to ensure that Cain gets back into the presence of God. God never mentions that Cain's family must not be bitter or hold unforgiveness. I'm not suggesting that we, as victims, become bitter and unforgiving. I'm suggesting that the church condemn the perpetrator instead of the victim. I'm suggesting that the church banishes the abuser without lecturing the victim on all the ways he or she isn't reconciling with him or trying to restore the marriage.

Abraham and Sarah

Abraham trafficked Sarah, as told in Genesis 20. This is such a twisted story. First, Abraham and Sarah were half-siblings. They had the same father but different mothers. Nowadays, that would be incest, but at that time, apparently it was OK. So, after Sodom and Gomorrah were destroyed, Abraham, Sarah, and all their livestock moved to Gerar. Abimelech, King of Gerar, saw how beautiful Sarah was and wanted her for his wife. So, Abraham gave her to the king and told him she was available because she was his sister. Sarah went along with it and affirmed that she was Abraham's sister. Note Sarah's submission to her husband here. God then makes the king and all his women infertile and tells King Abimelech in a dream that he was a dead man because he'd taken another man's wife. The king confronted Abraham, who excused himself by saying that Sarah *was* his sister and that he'd been afraid the king would kill him so he could take his wife. Sarah's excuse was that Abraham told her what to say. So, in today's language, Abe knew he had a gorgeous babe, and his archrival wanted her, so Abe gave his girl to his rival so the rival didn't shoot him up.

How does all that relate to domestic violence?

1. Sarah was treated as a possession with no mind, will, thought, or decision-making ability of her own. At the time, and in that culture, that was the woman's lot. My question is, are women in abusive relationships treated that way now? Are we treated as possessions? Not allowed to think or act on our own? Not allowed to have a job or any kind of independence? As victims, do we suffer consequences if we violate these rules that have been forced upon us? Is it made clear to us what we can and cannot say or talk about?

    While it's possible that victims don't have all these things happening at once, it's certainly likely that some, if not all, of these happen frequently. I realize that this may sound like "women's lib." To many, it may be completely blasphemous to insinuate that women should be allowed independence or the ability to act without first consulting with the man of the house. In fact, if it seems they do, snide comments are made about "who wears the pants in the family." Isn't it possible that a man can love his wife *and* allow her to make decisions without him? If our husband goes out and gets a good job, we congratulate him, support him, and celebrate his success. If we go out and get a job, the abusive husband considers that a threat. Why didn't we ask him first? What if he doesn't want us to get a job—doesn't the Bible say we're supposed to be keepers of the home? Don't we want to do what the Bible says?

    There was a time that we, as a small church group, went together to a different church in support of a gentleman we'd recently met. My husband was asked to stand and give a testimony. It was all one big lie. Many people approached him afterward and exclaimed over his faith and what a wonderful testimony that was. People told me how lucky I was to have such a man for a husband. As a victim at the time, I knew he was lying, and I also knew I had to be a submissive wife and not say a word. I knew I could not blow his cover or make him look bad to these new people we met. I was not allowed to think or act on my own. It was clear what I was and was not allowed to talk about to these people. Does this make me a good Christian wife or an accomplice who's complicit in the lies?

Afterward, I spoke to my church elder and told him there wasn't a shred of truth to anything my husband had said, and I gave examples to prove it. The men in our fellowship confronted my husband. "Do you want me to go back next week and tell them I didn't speak the truth?" my husband asked calmly. No remorse, no guilt, no acknowledgement that lying was wrong, no denial. Just a calm acceptance that he was found out, so should he go back and tell them he was lying? To a man, the men in the fellowship said no. The men in the fellowship agreed to uphold the lies. My husband's conscience didn't seem bothered at all. He just said he'd return next Sunday and say he hadn't told the truth, and *all the men said no!*

2. Self-preservation. Abraham was all about self-preservation, even to the point of putting his wife in a position to commit adultery and deceiving the king so that he and he alone would be safe. Was he acting in Sarah's best interest? Was he thinking of anybody except himself?

This reminds me so much of my husband wanting me to sleep closest to the bedroom door. Abusers, especially those with narcissistic traits or personality disorders, have an inordinately high opinion of themselves and their value to the world. Their safety is of the utmost importance, and they don't care about anyone else. It's rather difficult to follow the Scriptural

admonition for men to love their wives as Christ loved the church when the most important person to himself is himself.
3. Once again, God directly intervenes on behalf of the victim. He warned the king, who then took Sarah back in such a way that the responsibility was put directly on Abraham, the abuser. Notice that He didn't wait for Abraham to confess his wrongdoing. Nor did God wait for the king to figure out that everybody had become infertile since Sarah showed up. No. God told the other victim (the king) directly that he'd been the victim of a scam and that Abraham was responsible. God threatened the king with his life and told him to take Sarah (the main victim) back where she belonged. In all this, God protected Sarah, put the king in his place so he couldn't harm Abraham or Sarah, and brought Abraham's sin out in the open for everybody to see.
4. Open and public confrontation of a sinful situation tends to help curtail the possibility of it happening again. This reinforces my position that when victims are silent, the abuse continues. It's so important to speak out, to bring it out in the open. But again, just as God demonstrated, you must have a safety plan. Notice how God protected Sarah by going to the king and telling him God would kill him unless he gave her back to Abraham. His safety plan was to threaten the king with his death, so the king wouldn't harm Sarah. And He, God Himself, put all the responsibility on Abraham, so Abraham could not blame Sarah or be angry with her for betraying him. He completely humiliated Abraham, another key component of controlling abusive behavior. The abuser needs to feel the respect of others, and any threat of exposure humiliates him. He'll avoid that humiliation at all costs.

Saul and David

Consider Saul and David. David was married to Saul's daughter, which made him part of the family, which makes the Saul-David interactions fall into the category of domestic violence. Much of the account is relayed in 1 Samuel 2, which illustrates several things:

1. Mental Illness. It's clear in this passage that Saul was afflicted with a mental illness. It's also clear that it was sent by God because of Saul's poor behavior. Furthermore, the mental illness made Saul highly unpredictable and unstable. He vacillated between whether to kill David or not kill David, about being angry with David or not being angry, about being repentant or not repentant, etc. Any victim of domestic violence recognizes this behavior, the back and forth, flip-flopping on things that seem random and insignificant but are super important for fleeting moments to the abuser. It's also significant to note that Saul's son Jonathan didn't understand Saul and his abusive behavior as David did. David knew when Saul was likely to be abusive and told Jonathan, but Jonathan didn't agree and even argued with David that his father wouldn't hurt him.
Keep this example in mind. Other people will hear your story and will disagree and deny that what you're saying could be true. But no one knows your abuser like you do. Don't be swayed from your assessment when people don't listen to you. They don't know your abuser like you do. They won't agree and may even argue with you. But what would have happened if David had listened to Jonathan? He probably would have been killed. Jonathan was wrong.

2. Wisdom of Running and Hiding. David repeatedly ran and hid from Saul, even over several years. His wife first told him to run and hide, then Jonathan told him to run and hide. His army of soldiers helped hide him. God, Himself, warned David and hid him from Saul. Running and hiding is a safety plan. Communication through third parties is a safety plan. Keeping yourself separated from your abuser is a safety plan. All these things are evident in the account of David and Saul.
3. Having Friends Help Plan for Your Safe Exit. The priest Ahimelech and all the inhabitants of Nob illustrate this principle when David and his army are running from Saul. As they were fleeing, the men were very hungry and needed food. David stopped at the temple and asked the priest for the holy bread consecrated to the Lord—not meant for anyone to eat. He didn't tell the priest they were fleeing from the king or that the king intended to kill David. The priest gave the food to David and his men. Later, Saul arrived at the temple and learned the priest had fed David. So, Saul killed everyone there.

    David hadn't told the priest the truth. Had he told the truth, would the priest and the people have lived? We don't know. No one knows if they would have helped David if he'd told them the truth.

    When you, as a victim, ask anyone for help, make sure they understand the circumstances and risks. They need to have a safety plan as well and be on the lookout for the abuser and watch for clues to the abuser's intentions.
4. The Innocent Victim vs. Unprovoked Abuser. People may say things like, "It takes two," or, "There are two sides to every story," or that one person's story seems legitimate until you hear the other side. But we can

learn from the tale of David and Saul that it's possible for the victim to be innocent of wrongdoing and for the abuser to be 100 percent guilty. While Saul was actively seeking to kill David—for no reason—Saul actively called on God and asked the people to inquire of the Lord. He acted just like a true believer does when trying to follow the ways of God.

Your abuser can and might do exactly that. Mine did. He always had a Bible in his hand, and he always wanted to do a Bible study. As the account of Saul illustrates, however, Saul's reasons for "inquiring of the Lord" were to do evil against David, and God protected David. He spoke to David through the Ephod. He frustrated Saul's plans. He sent the Philistines to attack Saul's territory while Saul was hunting David—all to get Saul to drop the chase. But God didn't immediately deliver David from Saul. David ran from his oppressor for years. He feared for his life for years.

This can also be true for many victims, especially those in the church. You may think that because your abuser calls on the name of the Lord that it means they're true believers. Saul wasn't. Neither is anyone who abuses you. You may think that because you have a marital covenant, you must stay close, live with your abuser, continue marital relations, and put yourself in harm's way daily. This isn't what the account of David and Saul teaches.

Nabal and Abigail

This is another interesting situation that is found in 1 Samuel 25. David and his men protected Nabal's flocks and shepherds while they were all in the hills together. When it came time to shear the sheep and celebrate the harvest of wool, David sent his men to approach Nabal with humility to remind him of their services and to ask for some food as payment. Nabal was a very wealthy man, but he insulted David and all his men by sending the men away hungry. When David's men returned to him, they told him about Nabal's behavior, and David was mad as a wet hen. He told four hundred men to get their swords and come with him to annihilate the house of Nabal.

Nabal's servants, in the meantime, were alarmed by how Nabal treated David's men, and they ran to tell Nabal's wife, Abigail. She instantly recognized the deep trouble they were in and took significant action to save her household. She packaged up a lot of food and headed out to meet David. When she met him on the road, she bowed to the ground, told him her husband was a worthless fool, took responsibility for his actions, gave David lavish amounts of food, and reminded him that the unjust, foolish, and sinful behavior of Nabal couldn't justify David behaving the same way. She said David would one day be king, and he should not let hasty and wrong decisions become something he would regret later.

The lesson in this story is what Abigail tells David. Someone else's unjust, foolish, and sinful behavior doesn't justify the same behavior in return. Regardless of what our abuser does, we are never justified in returning evil for evil. This is so hard sometimes—so, so, so, so hard. But Abigail is right. We cannot stoop to the behavior of our abusers just because they behave badly toward us. In New Testament language, we must be beyond reproach.

> *Someone else's unjust, foolish, and sinful behavior doesn't justify the same behavior in return.*

This account is about the interaction between David, Nabal, and then Abigail, so it might not seem like a story about domestic violence. But think about what was *not* said and how the characters responded. Nabal insulted David. This wasn't the first time he'd insulted people. It happened so often that the servants immediately ran to Abigail to tell her about it. Abigail then set out to make the situation right. She'd been down this road before. She's had to cover for him in the past. Clearly, she wasn't concerned about the "submit to your husband in all things" teaching. She met David and told him that her husband was a total idiot. He was a stupid fool. Do wives, especially Old Testament wives, say that? She knew how abusive and horrid her husband was and decided she wouldn't be an accomplice anymore. She wouldn't comply with the murder of her entire family because her husband was an abusive jerk. She decided to "tell it like it is" and gave David sage advice that had always kept her from being corrupted by her husband's abuse.

There are a couple of takeaways from this story:

1. We don't need to make excuses for our abuser, try to keep his reputation untarnished, work to cover for him, or try to make him look good. Abigail just lays it out there. She tells David that her husband is a stupid fool.
2. We need to let God handle whatever discipline, vengeance, and retribution He decides is appropriate when He decides it's appropriate. Abigail never seemed to think of herself or how anything could benefit her other than saving the lives of her entire household. She treated David's men with the abundance and gratitude they deserved, and she wanted to keep David from doing something he would regret while keeping her family and household safe. She had no idea that one day, she would become the wife of the king, which happens when Nabal dies at God's hand shortly afterward. Her concerns weren't about herself or her self-interest. Her actions were meant to benefit others.

3. Just because your abuser thinks they have complete control over you, that doesn't mean that he does or that he has to, or that he can, or that you have to agree to that. Abigail didn't consult her husband. She didn't tell him what she was doing. She didn't tell him what she'd done until the next morning, and when she told him how close they'd come to being executed by the future king, Nabal had either a stroke or a heart attack. In short, God killed him. God took vengeance—not Abigail and not David.

Amnon and Tamar

Amnon and Tamar were David's children, and their story is told in 2 Samuel 13. These two were half-siblings in the royal family. Tamar was Absalom's full sister. Amnon had lusted after Tamar so much that he made himself sick. An advisor told him to pretend he was physically ill, and when the king came to see him, he should tell the king to send Tamar to bake him some food. So, the plan unfolded, and Tamar came to make food. Then Amnon sent everyone away and tried to rape Tamar. She said no; he should ask the king to let them marry, but Amnon raped her anyway. Then he despises her and sends her away in shame. Absolom has Tamar stay with him in his house, and he plots revenge for two years. After that, he conspired with other members of the royal household to kill Amnon, which he did.

Notice how the abuser despised and hated his victim. This is actually what happens. She tried to give him what he wanted, but it wasn't enough. He took what he wanted without any regard for how he could legitimately have the thing he said he wanted. This is what abusers do. They want to be happy and think if they get this or that from the victim, they'll be happy. So, they take what they want from the victim, even though the victim knows that anything he takes will not fulfill his need. In the end, the abuser despises and hates the victim, which, in turn, results in further abuse. Each time the victim tries to give what the abuser needs or thinks they need, the abuser doesn't receive it. Instead, the abuser takes and then despises and hates.

Let me tell you a story. One time, we had strawberries growing on a hillside. The hill was very steep, and I was concerned that when my husband mowed the lawn, he would slip on the grass, and his foot would go under the lawnmower blades. So, I planted strawberries there. My husband entered the kitchen one day and said, "There are a bunch of ripe strawberries." Because I knew him, I knew that he was really saying, "Go out and pick the strawberries." This is an example of his manipulation. A short time later, I went outside and picked the strawberries. I washed them, cut them, sugared them, and put them in the fridge so we could have them later. I hadn't picked very many because the ones that looked ripe from a distance were still green on the underside.

That evening, we went to a neighbor's house to swim. To get there, we walked past the strawberry patch. My husband turned to me, irritated, and loudly said, "I said there were a bunch of ripe strawberries!" The entire time we were at the neighbor's, he was grumpy about the strawberries. I told him I'd picked them, and they were in the fridge, ready to eat. He didn't believe me and said I was lying. As we walked home, he angrily stomped ahead, got to the strawberry patch, and started looking through them. Sure enough, he couldn't find any ripe ones. That made him even more angry. He went into the house, looked in the fridge, saw the strawberries, slammed the fridge door, and silently stomped off. He thought he'd be happy if I picked the strawberries, but instead, he despised me for doing what he asked.

Nothing else is ever said about Tamar except that Absolom names one of his daughters after her. We do know that

Absalom took care of his sister. We know that she was kept safe from Amnon. But that's all we know. Our greatest lesson in this instance is that *no contact* is sometimes the best way to go. Tamar was never again exposed to Amnon, expected to go see him, told to forgive him, encouraged to reconcile the relationship, etc. It appears they never interacted again. In my experience, no contact is the only way to begin healing.

Tamar's illustration is the only one where God, Himself, doesn't directly intervene. And this is a lesson for you, too. There will be many times when it doesn't seem that God is here, that God knows, that God cares, or that God has any interest in you. But I encourage you that even in the darkest times when it seems God is nowhere and you are all alone with evil beyond what you can bear, God never leaves you. Never. He will work to show you He is with you. He may not take you out of the situation when you want Him to but never doubt for a moment that He is with you. He will never leave you. Look for Him, and He will show Himself to you everywhere.

> *Even in the darkest times when it seems God is nowhere and you are all alone with evil beyond what you can bear, God never leaves you. Never.*

Another story: After I handed my husband over to Satan, I asked my husband for a time of prayer and fasting with no sex. I was granted that time. But after six weeks passed, it was over. I couldn't deprive my husband of my body for too long, right? So that very morning, he was all over me. It was about 5:30 or 6:00 a.m., and the children wouldn't be up until about 8:30 or 9:00. I saw no way out. I started shaking, and I felt nauseous. Seriously sick. Tears pricked my eyes. *This must be what women feel like when they know they're about to be raped*, I thought to myself. I prayed silently, *God, just get me through this. Just get me through it. Don't let me cry, and just get me through it.* Just as my husband was reaching for me, the phone rang. There were no cell phones back then, and our only phone was downstairs in the kitchen. I held my breath. *Who could be calling this early in the morning?* I thought to myself. The phone kept ringing. Finally, my husband got up, wrapped himself in something, and went down to answer the phone. It was a gentleman we scarcely knew who'd been to our church fellowship a few times. He kept my husband on the phone for a long time—until the children started getting up. God *did* deliver me, even though I didn't ask for that. God is always there.

10

What Does the Church Believe About Domestic Violence?

I believe in the Bible and that Jesus Christ is my Lord and Savior. I respect everyone's right to have their beliefs, and this book is in no way attempting to influence anyone's beliefs, but since I'm a Christian, I can only speak about domestic violence from that viewpoint. However, the Muslim faith is not known for treating women well. Neither is the religious and social structure of many Asian countries. So, for those who aren't Christians, please read on because much of what I say may also apply to you and your household of faith. But for Christians especially, this is for you.

When we contemplate The Church, what comes to mind? Maybe the great history of faith. Maybe the beautiful cathedrals of old. Maybe stories of martyrs. Maybe your own church family and the community it provides. Maybe you have favorite pastors, teachers, nuns, or other leaders in the church who were important to you at one time or another. Whatever comes to mind, we certainly don't want to think that domestic violence is a part of it.

As humans, we compartmentalize. This is this, and that is that, and they don't cross over. Domestic violence, we think, doesn't happen in the church—not in *my* church! And yet, statistics for domestic violence in the church are the same, and probably worse, than those outside the church. According to the article "Domestic Abuse: 4 Things Pastors and Churches Need to Know" by *Baptist Churches of New England* (bcne.net), published August 16, 2021, not only does domestic violence happen just as much inside the church as outside, but church women also stayed in it an average of 3.5 years longer.

I was talking with a Mormon friend about domestic violence, and he told me how the Mormon faith was structured so that domestic violence simply doesn't occur. Then within a week or two, it came out that a staff member in the White House during the Trump administration was divorcing for the second time because of domestic violence against both his first and second wives. He was a Mormon.

> *Statistics for domestic violence in the church are the same, and probably worse than, those outside the church.*

Unfortunately, this attitude of "it can't happen here" allows domestic violence to flourish under our noses. We see no evil, hear no evil, speak no evil, so that must mean there is no evil! Silence keeps victims imprisoned. Next time you're in church, count four women down the pews or seats. According to the article, "1-in-4 Highly Religious U.S. Marriages Have Abuse," from *Life-Saving Divorce* (lifesavingdivorce.com), one of those four women is physically or sexually abused by her partner. Count four men. Statistically, one of those four is physically or sexually abusing his partner. Multiply that by all the men and women in the church. According to an article published on the website verywellmind.com entitled, "How Domestic Violence Varies by Ethnicity" by Buddy T, published April 26, 2021, ethnicities that are non-white have as high as a 40 percent incidence rate. It's even higher for the LGBTQ+ community.

The churches I've attended put such an emphasis on the headship of the husband and the submissive role of the wife that I believe domestic violence in the church is higher than outside the church. A good Christian wife won't talk to people about how badly her husband treats her. She's learned to forgive, turn the other cheek, and respect her husband. So, the reported incidence of domestic violence would be lower for this reason.

Furthermore, the pastors I've encountered prefer to treat domestic violence as something that can be handled with a few marriage counseling sessions, usually with him acting as the counselor. They speak gently about the passages instructing the husband to love his wife and remind the wife to submit to her husband. The husband usually agrees and is his most charming and affable self during the meeting with the pastor. The pastor is then satisfied that the husband is clear on his role and that the wife will work on her submission, and another troubled marriage is on the mend. It's certainly not domestic violence, just a troubled marriage that needs a few counseling sessions or perhaps a marriage retreat or conference.

When wives speak to their pastors privately, the pastor's first counsel often comes straight out of the Bible: Submit to your husband. If he isn't happy with you, you're told, it must be because you aren't submitting well enough. Make his favorite food, he tells you, have lots of sex, wear things he likes, and keep the house clean and the children happy. Next come his admonitions to forgive, to not be bitter, and to overlook offenses. Be sure to take the log out of your eye, he says, before you complain about the speck in his. What possible log could I have that would make my abuser's abuse a speck?

IS THIS DOMESTIC ABUSE?

Pastors and teachers have said these things to me. They said that since I kept coming to them, I was obviously not working on submitting to my husband, and if I continued in this manner, they wouldn't see me anymore. This put the responsibility for the abuse on *me*. What clergy don't realize when they admonish an abused woman is that the abuse is *not* her responsibility. It's not her responsibility that it's happening, and it's not her responsibility to try to make it stop.

Say, for example, a store owner is stocking his shelves. A robber comes in, shoots up the place, takes the cash from the register, and leaves. The owner calls the police. While the police are there, the robber comes back. The shop owner says, "That's him! That's the guy who robbed my store!" The police ask the robber if he robbed the store. The guy says, "No, of course not!" So, the police turn to the owner and tell him he must be mistaken and needs to forgive this guy. If he doesn't, God won't forgive him, and he may go to hell. He might want to start setting money out on the counter for the "alleged" robber; then, he won't have to shoot the place up. Remember, the Bible says if a man asks for your shirt, you should give him your coat as well. Additionally, he should talk with the "alleged" robber about what he wants and then do it for him: order the things he wants, maybe have cute girls working the counter, and of course, leave the cash out and available for him. If he could also go with the "alleged" robber to counseling, he might be better able to deal with his bitterness toward the "alleged" robber. As an officer of the law, the officers would be happy to serve as a counselor, but only if the objective is to completely restore the relationship. Since the officer is so sincere and serious about what he's saying, the shop owner is rightly confused and wonders if he's dreaming or if this is an actual, serious discussion—because the officer is not doing his job.

To a victim of domestic violence, this is what it sounds like when she goes to the pastor for help. He misses the point and is, therefore, completely unhelpful, and nothing he says makes any sense. By changing the scenario to a store owner and robber story, can you see that the advice many pastors give is an admission that the abuse is occurring? Why would the police officer tell the shopkeeper to lay money on the counter if he thought the robber was innocent? In like manner, why would a pastor give you suggestions for making your husband stop abusing you if he believed there was no abuse?

Who's the Expert on the Abuse?

This brings us to our next question: Who is the expert on the abuse? When an abused individual seeks the advice of the pastoral staff, and they're told to work harder to be better so the abuser will be happier—or forgive or else they won't be forgiven and will go to hell—what false message is communicated to the victim? There are lots of them, such as:

- The victim can control the abuse through their behavior.
- If the victim behaves right, the abuse will stop because the abuser will be happier.
- The abuse isn't the issue. The issue is that the victim isn't working hard enough and isn't forgiving enough.
- The abuser doesn't need to change anything; the victim needs to change.
- The victim is in danger of hellfire if she doesn't be quiet, forgive, and keep trying to submit to her husband.

These are all lies. The real issue is *the abuse!* What's happening behind closed doors? How does it compare with standard definitions of the six recognized forms of abuse: physical, sexual, emotional, verbal, financial, and spiritual? Who is the only one who can clearly state what is happening to her and possibly the children? The victim. The victim is the only one who knows the truth about the situation.

Who Do You Believe and Why?

The victim's story will be very different from the abuser's story. Once when I was talking about my situation, a pastor by training didn't realize I was talking about my family, and he said, "Well, women lie." All the pastors I've ever contacted about my situation said they wanted my husband and me to meet with him together. That puts an impossible burden on both the pastor and the victim. Perpetrators are incredibly charming and liars beyond belief. They will spin any story to get anyone to believe what they say. They will purposely act astoundingly repentant just to get the blessing of the pastor, so they can go home and rip the victim to shreds. The most important thing anyone can do when domestic violence is mentioned is to believe the expert witness—the victim.

The single, most important thing anyone can do when domestic violence is mentioned is to believe the expert witness—the victim.

Yes, there are times when women lie. No doubt. But considering that anywhere between 30 percent and 50 percent of the congregation is suffering from domestic violence and roughly 90 percent of the time women are the reporting victims of physical and sexual abuse, it's pretty safe to believe her and start acting accordingly. If it's later revealed that she was lying, there will be time to deal with that then. But if a churchgoing woman approaches church staff about domestic violence, you can be sure she's suffered in silence for a long time, and it's taken great courage and risk for her to speak. She knows her husband will consider this an act of deepest rebellion, disrespect, and betrayal, which could be very dangerous for her.

Why Churchgoers, Pastors, and Staff Believe Domestic Violence Isn't in Their Church

There was a time when a visiting preacher spoke on marriage and how to have a good one. He spoke on love and respect, forgiveness, and yielding to the other. He talked about giving and not expecting. He talked about trust and always believing the best in the other person. I went to him after the service and told him I came from an abusive marriage. His entire countenance changed. He apologized to me and said, "I'm not in any way talking about abusive situations. That's completely different, and my teaching does not apply."

I was shocked. I'd never had a pastor speak to me about abuse that way. He told me he'd grown up in an abusive home. His father was very involved in church and was very physically abusive to his mother, his brother, and him. He said no one at church believed him, and he got in trouble for slandering his father, who then beat the living tar out of him when he found out what he'd said. As a child, he learned that church people couldn't be trusted to protect the innocent. He said that he can't preach about everything when he's preaching, so he tries to preach to the majority, which is understandable. But what is the majority?

I suspect that the reasons for ignoring domestic violence in the church are related to the psychology—or mindset—of those of us in the church. We like to think that churchgoers wouldn't do such a thing. We may struggle with things like losing patience with the children, speeding on the highway, or being angry at our mother-in-law, so we don't let her see her grandchildren—fairly benign things. Surely people in the church don't murder anyone or rape women and children. But when you hear about domestic violence in the news, you find pastors trafficking the girls in their youth group, fathers murdering whole families, husbands, wives, boyfriends, and girlfriends killing each other and committing suicide, etc. Every sort of ill we don't want to think happens in the church happens in the church.

I remember listening to Hank Hanegraaff's radio show, *The Bible Answer Man*, years ago. A woman called in because her husband was a physically violent alcoholic and womanizer, and she didn't think she could take it anymore. Hank asked her if she had gone to her pastor about it. She replied, "He *is* the pastor." To Hank's credit, he immediately went to a commercial break, and when the ad was over, they started a re-run of a previous episode. I hope that meant he was being supportive and helpful to this desperate woman.

Perhaps we ignore domestic violence in the church because we have a distorted and unrealistic view of the people in the church. But I think it goes deeper than that. Suppose we admit that 50 percent of the people, including the pastors, suffer from domestic violence in the home. In that case, we simultaneously must admit that it's been happening in our church with or without our knowledge, and we've done nothing. We've let this evil happen under our noses and haven't seen it. We haven't seen it because we don't want to see it, and we haven't seen it because the abusers work to keep it hidden. If someone at your church were to tell you her husband abuses her, how would you respond? Be honest with yourself. Would you be awkward? Would you not know what to say? Would you tell her she should talk to the pastor? Would you give a compassionate smile or hug, ask

Every sort of ill we don't want to think happens in the church, happens in the church.

if there's anything you can do, and tell her that you'll pray for her? Would you get away from the conversation as quickly as possible? Would you tell her she should call the police? Would you question whether you should believe her or wonder what she did to cause it? It's my most fervent prayer that reading this book will give you an understanding and tools to help her and all the others like her.

There *are* some things you could do. First, sit her down someplace at that moment, and ask her to tell you everything. If it takes six hours, drop your plans for the day, find her a babysitter, or go to Starbucks or a safe place to listen. Ask questions. No advice, no condemnation, no telling her God hates divorce. Listen. Get her a decent meal. Ask for examples. Seek to understand. Cry with her because I guarantee she will cry. She will probably cry just because you listened to her.

Then follow up with her. Call her. Talk about the abuse and find out how she is doing. Eventually, she'll probably let something slip out that she needs. Her car needs repairs. Her phone quit charging. The seasons are changing, and she only has $100 to clothe the children for the winter. She's been locked out of the bank accounts and can't go grocery shopping. Her mom is ill, but her abuser won't let her go visit her. When she lets something slip, wrack your brain to see if there is some way you can help with that thing.

Above all else, *do not say*, "Call me if there's anything I can do for you," unless you're actually going to do something for her when she asks. Saying, "I'll pray for you," only counts if you do something tangible as well. I can't tell you how many people knew about my struggle and offered to help, but when I told them how they could help me, they didn't do anything. They would say something like, "Yeah, let's do that." And nothing. Crickets. Most of the time, that was the last time they spoke to me.

The three gentlemen mentioned in my dedication are the exceptions to the rule. They not only offered help, but they also actually helped. And I can-

Saying, "I'll pray for you," only counts if you do something tangible as well.

not begin to say how incredible their help was and continues to be. The effects were profound, transformational, life-changing, and long-lasting, yet I would be willing to bet that each one doesn't feel like they did a lot. Never underestimate the effect your acts of kindness and service will have on the lives of domestic violence victims.

Are There Typical Behaviors?

What is typical behavior for an abused wife? What is the typical behavior of an abuser? People often think that if there's abuse, they should be able to see some visible evidence. While this is true in a very small minority of cases, remember that there are six recognized forms of domestic violence: physical, sexual, verbal, emotional, financial, and spiritual. Only in physical abuse will there be visible signs, and only if the physical abuse was violent enough, and only if the physical abuse was inflicted in places normally seen, like the face or hands. All other areas can be kept covered and out of sight.

Neither the abused nor the abuser will be obvious to the casual observer. In fact, they won't be obvious to anyone else for a long time. Family and friends are slowly but surely distanced from the victim, and the victim is steadily more isolated. The victim loves her abuser and doesn't want people to think badly about him. She believes him when he gives her gifts in the honeymoon phase of the domestic violence circle and tells her that he loves her and is sorry. She believes him when he says he's under so much stress or pressure. She wants to be a good wife, so she accepts the blame when he says she deserves the abuse. After all, it takes two, right? And she needs to own up to her responsibilities, he tells her. The woman is ashamed and thinks she deserves such treatment. So, nobody says anything.

So, what does an abuser look like? *They look just like everyone else.* When researching homicides in the news, I found that a significant portion of the time, nobody had any clue that something was amiss. Occasionally, articles stated that neighbors sometimes heard them fighting or coworkers said the guy had a temper. Still, most of the time, when family, friends, or neighbors made a statement, they said they had no idea there was a problem.

How would church people expect a church-going abuse victim to look, speak, act, and behave? What about a church-going abuser? It's ridiculous that people would think abusers or their victims should look any different than anyone else. Domestic violence is a sin. People do their very best to hide sin so it goes undetected. It makes sense that no one knows. Everyone puts on their happy face and goes to church with all the other perfect-looking people, and we all pretend that everyone is always holy.

> *Domestic violence is a sin. People do their very best to hide sin so it goes undetected.*

Occasionally, a brave soul will confess a sinful habit, appear to repent, and try to change. Often, this is a real experience, and the confessor goes on to conquer the habit with the help of God. Abusive people, however, will use this ploy to gain the support of the pastoral staff and the congregation. That must mean he's sincere since he publicly wept tears of repentance. The humility it took for him to confess before witnesses—praise God! You can see the compassion and sympathy oozing from everyone watching the display. And then they come to you afterward and tell you what a wonderful person your abuser is. The sorrow leading to repentance was so obvious. Victims must believe this repentance is real and give them time to overcome the habit. Again. And again. And again. This is strictly manipulation to trick the congregation and pastoral staff into enabling the abuse to continue. Once again, the victim suffers while the abuser has no consequences or accountability. If the abuser starts feeling too much heat, he may decide the family needs to find a new church home. A wife can't tell her husband no about something like that. He's not asking her to sin, so she must submit. So, the cycle starts over again, and the abuse continues unchecked.

If there are any signs of abuse at all, they will barely be noticeable. Look for very, very subtle clues, such as:

- The victim drops her eyes to the floor a lot.
- The abuser interrupts the victim, correcting or finishing what she says.
- He may give her "looks," after which she no longer speaks.
- The abuser may say mildly or blatantly insulting or condescending things to her and then carry on with other people without a thought.
- The abuser will chastise, correct, complain about, or belittle the victim publicly.
- The abuser may overreact to things the victim says or does.
- The abuser may give the victim and others the silent treatment when upset about something.

Keep your eyes open for abuse in your church. You may be the victim's only lifeline.

11

Standard Doctrinal Statements and the Role of the Clergy

So, what is the role of the pastor? First, it's not to counsel. At the risk of ruffling feathers, pastors are not trained counselors, and domestic violence is way beyond their skill level. Domestic violence is a complex mix of mental illness, a culture of violence in the perpetrator, dysfunctional behaviors, and enabling behaviors developed by the perpetrator and the network of surrounding individuals—including the victim and the church—that keeps the abuse going and escalating.

The primary role of the pastor is support and education. And he can educate himself by asking these questions: What's happening at home? How does it fit into the recognized forms of abuse? Where are they on the cycle of violence? Are there children involved, and to what extent? What support systems does the victim have? Is she seeing a counselor? What resources is she aware of to help her? Does she have money and transportation? Has she talked with anyone about developing a safe exit strategy? Has she consulted an attorney? Has law enforcement been notified? Is there a gun in the home? Has there been stalking or harassment in the workplace? Has she been becoming increasingly isolated? What resources can the church body offer? Is there someone who can act as a point of contact who will regularly check in with the victim, who will be on call in case of emergency, and who will be willing to take the victim to the emergency room, police station, or a DV shelter should the need arise?

The pastor should know the congregation's members well enough to reach out for things like emergency childcare, a meal chain, security systems, a used car, storage of personal valuables, or paying for counseling. So many small things can take the stress off the victim and allow her to start formulating a plan for moving forward. Ideally, there should be a board of qualified individuals in the church body who are willing to assist on a pro bono basis in a variety of areas: counseling, legal assistance, financial budgeting and planning, offering a used car or rental home for free on a temporary basis, etc.

I've never been in a single church that has any documentation or mention anywhere, ever, of domestic violence and what it is. This is a scourge that affects a large percentage of any given congregation. Between the six recognized forms, there are only statistics on physical and sexual abuse. At a minimum, 25 percent to 30 percent of each congregation is affected by those. One study that attempted to isolate emotional/psychological abuse found that 50 percent of men and women suffered. In addition, there's verbal, financial, and spiritual abuse with no documented studies or statistics, yet we know they exist. If a minimum of 25 percent to 30 percent suffer from physical and/or sexual abuse and 50 percent suffer from emotional abuse, it's a safe bet that at least 50 percent of any given congregation experiences domestic violence. If 50 percent of your church family, this week, were diagnosed with cancer, here are some likely responses by the church:

- Offer home visitations
- Offer help to caregivers
- Conduct seminars on cancers and how to avoid known causes or things that increase the risk of getting cancers
- Invite speakers on alternative ways to beat cancer and self-care/self-help for those who are ill
- Sponsor fundraisers or other ways to financially benefit those with mounting medical bills
- Solicit donations of supplies and medical equipment for the sick
- Go to the federal or state governments to find out why the large numbers of cancers are occurring and press for investigations to take care of the problem

The church finds many ways to help when a great many are afflicted. But somehow, even though the numbers are large, the church doesn't do much regarding domestic violence. Sometimes, churches align themselves with a shelter and give a portion of their donations or hold fundraisers for the shelter, but if we look at the list above, could the church do these same things and adapt them for domestic violence situations? Why not teach about it during the service, youth group, and Sunday school? Why not give out information packets to everyone regularly that explain domestic violence, what it is, and what to do if you're suffering from it? Why not have a list of resources posted in the ladies' restrooms with phone numbers and contact information for services for victims? Why not have speakers and seminars not only on marriage but also on domestic violence? Why not have workshops on how to keep your marriage from becoming abusive, self-defense strategies, and how to keep yourself from enabling abuse? Why not believe the victim or the children when they speak about it? Why not have denomination-wide conferences teaching pastors and pastoral staff about domestic violence and how to handle it? Don't forget that pastors and pastoral staff contribute equally to the statistics.

Church Doctrine and How It Hurts the Victims

What standard church doctrine, used as instruction, hurts an abused person? An abusive person?

Doctrine	What the Victim Hears
1. Divorce is not an option.	You are completely stuck in this marriage and have no options. Even if he commits adultery or harms you or the children in any way, your responsibility is to forgive, turn the other cheek, and bless.
2. Have a meek and quiet spirit.	Be quiet and be happy about it.
3. Win your spouse without a word.	If you want your partner's treatment of you to improve, keep your mouth shut and treat him like a king.
4. Wives submit to your husband in all things as unto the Lord.	Do what he says—no matter how you feel about it or what you think about it.
5. The wife must respect her husband.	As the head of the home, the man has absolute authority regarding everything.
6. Patriarchy	You will want to be in charge, but you can't.
7. Your desire shall be for your husband, who shall rule over you.	"Yes, sir," and instant obedience is appropriate.

I hope you can see that these doctrinal positions don't protect victims of abuse or uncover abuses or call abusers to accountability or acknowledge that the man of the house could be doing something contrary to Biblical teaching. There's no way for a victim to even inquire about his behaviors that are confusing or hurtful. There's no place in these doctrinal positions for her to confront her husband about non-Biblical behavior.

In a healthy marriage, these seven doctrines don't represent how a husband and wife live. They love God and each other; there's give and take, compromise, negotiation, sacrifice, love, mutual respect, kindness, yielding, and thinking of the other more highly than self. So, people in a healthy marriage might read the list and say, "That's not the way it is." And they'd be correct.

But we aren't talking about healthy marriages. We're talking about abusive ones. And whether people want to admit it or not, these messages are what's communicated to a victim of abuse—not only by her husband but also by the church.

I'd like to dwell on the patriarchy for just a moment. This was an important doctrine in our church and household. It was inspired by a seminar we went to by Bill Gothard and the Institute in Basic Life Principles. Years later, Bill Gothard was sued in 2014 and 2016 for sex abuse and harassment claims from over thirty women. The idea of patriarchy was instilled in boys by teaching that they had authority over women because, eventually, they'd be the head of the house and could do whatever they wanted. So, it only made sense to begin practicing that authority before marriage.

This made for some interesting conflicts. In our little church fellowship, the older boys competed to be next in charge under the dads. It was ripe for bullying. And that's exactly what happened. The young man or men who were the bullies got their way. The bullied ones were expected to forgive and yield to the bully, who was reinforced in the bullying until the cycle escalated.

In 2021, Josh Duggar was indicted on child porn charges after being named as a child molester by his younger sisters and one of their friends in his teen years. Josh Duggar is the oldest son of Jim Bob and Michelle Duggar of TV fame, and it makes perfect sense. The Duggars also followed the patriarchal teaching. He was groomed by patriarchy to do whatever he wanted. He was taught that the oldest boy/the one in charge/the head of the house could do whatever he wanted. That's what patriarchy teaches.

While these concepts might steer a healthy couple toward a supportive relationship, that's not true in a domestic violence situation. The victim (a woman most of the time) goes to the pastor, and she hears these seven principles. She desperately wants them to work for her and does her best to implement them. The abuser doesn't care what the Bible says about what he should do. He takes these principles and runs with them. She must do everything he wants when he wants it, and she cannot say anything. That's what items 2, 3, and 4 in the chart on page 143 mean. If she doesn't like it, she's violating numbers 4 and 7. If she tries to speak up and defend herself, she's violating 2 and 3. If she tries negotiating or coming to some compromise, she's accused of violating number 6 and usurping his authority. And she can't even think about leaving. Divorce is not an option.

Multiple Christian leaders said that to me. For better or worse—till death do us part. Instead of a loving commitment, that phrase became a life sentence and a threat. Who did they think would be dying?

Does Standard Church Doctrine Match What God Says About Domestic Violence?

There are many denominations out there and many religious beliefs. I don't know them all. I can only go over the Scriptures and compare what Scripture says to the doctrinal statements I've heard, read, or been told. There are no accounts of domestic violence in the New Testament. But what we have in the New Testament are many admonitions regarding behavior, who we are to associate with, and what we are to distance ourselves from. There are many passages we could look at, but I want to focus on two statements:

1. Do not be unequally yoked with unbelievers.
2. Put away the evil person from among you.

Interestingly, both passages deal with marital situations as a context. Do not be unequally yoked to unbelievers is a direct instruction to those contemplating marriage. Don't marry someone who's an unbeliever. For those who don't want to be judgmental, how do you follow that instruction? I didn't judge my marriage partner, and I should have. I should have considered tiny red flag moments and evaluated them. Like when he pushed for sex, and I didn't want it. Like when he wanted to decide what I should or should not wear. Like when he wanted me to stop wearing makeup like the women in his Pentecostal upbringing but constantly compared how bad I looked with other hot young things in tight jeans and makeup. I should have been living my life more in accordance with what I said I believed. But once you are married, what then? There's a passage that states that if the unbeliever wishes to depart, let them depart. The believer in the pair is under no obligation to preserve the marriage. But here's the problem: What if the unbeliever refuses to depart? What then? This is the situation for many abuse victims.

The Church wants nothing but the restoration of the marriage. Unless there's been adultery, there are no grounds for divorce, so restoration of the marriage is the only alternative. And even if adultery exists, the victim is encouraged to forgive and remain in the marriage.

What about the passage that says to put the evil person away from you? Again, the context is marriage, with a man married to his father's wife (his mother or stepmother). Paul directly tells the believers in the church to get rid of him. This man claims to be a believer and goes to church with the rest of them, but Paul tells them to put him out of the church.

Does this create a precedent where if an individual is doing something wicked, the church should judge it as so and put him or her out of the church? The passage is silent about what should happen to the innocent family members. What about the children? Can they still go to Sunday school? What about the wife? Can she still attend and be welcomed into the fellowship? As we learned from the Old Testament accounts dealing with domestic violence, it appears that the wicked one needs to be banished, but the innocent family members are not, nor are they encouraged to remain in contact with the wicked one. Nor are they required to forgive or attempt to restore the relationship. The wickedness is banished, not the victims.

> *Does this create a precedent where if an individual is doing something wicked, the church should judge it as so and put him or her out of the church?*

The church required that I—the victim—submit, work on improving my Christianity, and seek to restore the marriage. The problem is that none of those things address the abuse or the abuser. The Bible tells me to put the evil person away from me and that I must not be yoked with unbelievers, yet the church told me I must submit to the evil person and that I couldn't be unyoked from the unbeliever.

In my experience, the church requires victims to demonstrate that they aren't bitter, unforgiving, vindictive, or seeking vengeance. Victims are required to accept responsibility for the reason for their abuse and are required—under the pain of hellfire—to publicly demonstrate forgiveness. There are no recorded instances in Scripture, anywhere, of God requiring such things of victims of domestic violence. I'm not saying that we should not forgive. I'm saying God doesn't require evidentiary proof, and neither should the church. God *does* require that the wicked person be banished and the victim protected from the wicked person. But the church does the exact opposite.

Interestingly, the Scriptural accounts don't give the wicked person the opportunity to repent. They're confronted, judged as wicked, and punished—banished like Cain, humbled like Abraham, and killed as Saul, Nabal, Amnon, and Ananias were. Saul and Amnon had time during which they could have repented and been given another chance. But they were not *given* time to apologize, repent, and ask for forgiveness. Again, the church does the opposite. It instructs sinners to repent and ask for forgiveness and pressures the victims to publicly announce the repentance as real and forgive.

Biblical accounts also focus on protecting the victim and keeping the victim(s) from further encounters with or harm from the wicked person. Hiding, third-party communication, moving away, no contact—all are tactics used to protect the victim from further harm. The church doesn't protect the victims but pressures them to continue to put themselves in harm's way. If victims balk or refuse, the church uses that as proof that the victim is bitter and unforgiving, and therefore, they're taken to task about their blind spots or lectured about how they're heading down the road to hell.

12

What Does the Church Need to Do Now?

I was told that the love passage in 1 Corinthians 13 is the most beautiful passage on love, and I needed to apply it to my spouse and my marriage. I needed to believe all things, hope all things, endure all things, and my love for my spouse must never fail. But here's a question: How was the *pastor* living that passage in relation to *me*? How do Christians live out that passage in relation to survivors of domestic violence? As a victim of abuse, how is it that I am the only one held to follow that passage in relation to my abuser, but no one is required to behave this way toward me as the victim of abuse?

Do pastors and pastoral staff have any formal training in domestic violence? What *do* pastors know about DV? How are they trained?

Interestingly, even though domestic violence can affect so many in each congregation, in a discussion with a seminary professor, I learned that a class or two in counseling is about as close to addressing domestic violence as seminaries get. So, we fill our seminarians' minds with unrealistic expectations about Christian families. We deny that sin is going on behind closed doors. We pronounce doctrinal statements from the pulpit and in private discussions with our pastors that are blatantly untrue for abusive situations. We refuse to teach our students about domestic violence, and then we send them out to lead congregations where at least a third of the congregants have a dire need that they have no idea exists and aren't prepared to handle.

The other critical issue is that pastors and pastoral staff are a part of the statistics. Pastors and their families also suffer from domestic violence. Missionaries and church leaders also suffer from domestic violence.

But when we get to leadership as perpetrators, there are greater issues to address. In a standard marital situation, domestic violence is about controlling the behavior and lives of the spouse and family; when someone in church leadership is the perpetrator, the stakes are higher because the spouse and family must preserve his image at all costs. The abuser will control his family and others in the church leadership. Using a tactic called triangulation, he will spin incredible lies and pit congregants and staff against each other to maintain control. He (or she, obviously) will intimidate others and accuse them of unfounded or distorted things to take them off their guard and put them on the defensive. They will keep their staff confused, using the same tactics a perpetrator uses in the home to maintain control.

> *When someone in church leadership is the perpetrator, the stakes are higher because the spouse and family must preserve his image at all costs.*

When control is exerted over large numbers of individuals, it gives the perpetrator such a sense of power that they begin to believe their power is divinely appointed. They'll slowly but steadily become increasingly blatant and corrupt, believing themselves to be above the laws of God and man. They're highly persuasive and forceful, and when allegations begin to escalate to denominational leaders, rather than being investigated and removed from their positions, they're often moved to a different place or given a different but no less dangerous position.

I have met the wife of such a man, a missionary who was put in charge of youth revivals both domestically and abroad. Even though his wife revealed what this man did to his family and the children at the youth retreats, denominational leadership continued to allow him to "serve the Lord." Finally, some youth from the revivals came forward publicly, and the man is now behind bars for life. Again, the wife wasn't believed or supported, and she and her daughter nearly died, only escaping by jumping out a bedroom window. With domestic violence, the wage of sin is death. And often, it's the death of the innocent victims, not the perpetrator.

Does the Church Consider Domestic Violence to Be a Legitimate Problem?

The upper echelons of denominational leadership need to prioritize domestic violence awareness and prevention rather than pretending it doesn't exist. I understand there's fear and pride in the charisma and work of the staff. But is it better to have the media get word of a story and disgrace the entire denomination—and Christendom in general—or to confront the violence one staff member at a time and eliminate the cancer internally?

It's not unlike the Catholic church scandal, where certain priests abused children in their parishes. Protecting the guilty causes more harm to the innocent! "Woe to those who call evil good, and good evil." "But whoever causes one of these little ones who believe in me to stumble, it would be better for him to have a heavy millstone hung around his neck and to be drowned in the depths of the sea." And again, "See that you do not despise one of these little ones, for I say to you that their angels in heaven continually see the face of my Father who is in heaven."

> *The upper echelons of denominational leadership need to prioritize domestic violence awareness and prevention rather than pretending it doesn't exist.*

Do we think that hiding the abuse on earth in the hopes that the dull-witted beneath us won't catch on goes unnoticed by God Almighty? It's He who we need to respect, honor, and fear, not the media or what will happen to the offering plate if the pastor gets exposed.

Pastor Ravi Zacharias is a high-profile example. Please see the article written by Daniel Silliman and Kate Shellnutt for *Christianity Today*, "Ravi Zacharias Hid Hundreds of Pictures of Women, Abuse During Massages, and a Rape Allegation."[3] There's such pride and arrogance there that it's shameful. Instead of hiding the abuse, the church should be hiding and protecting *the victims* while simultaneously judging and vehemently expelling the abuser—no matter what his position in the church.

How Does Pride Come into Play?

As a victim, it's been hard for me to accept the role I played. It's been hard to admit that my marriage is a disaster, which will probably have far-reaching effects on my grown children and

---

[3] https://www.christianitytoday.com/news/2021/february/ravi-zacharias-rzim-investigation-sexual-abuse-sexting-rape.html

future grandchildren if I'm ever blessed with any. It's been hard to admit that I didn't pay attention to red flags or confront things when they made me uncomfortable, and there were ramifications. Everything that's been hard for me to admit has been because of my pride. I didn't want a failed marriage. I didn't want to mess up in any way. I didn't want my children to be negatively impacted by anything I did. I didn't want there to be any negative consequences at all.

On a corporate level, the church is the same. Domestic violence is a blight. We don't want to admit it's in our church. We don't want to think that any of our members are abusers behind closed doors. We want to think that we only have minor issues in our congregation and that those with major issues are few and far between.

There's a vast difference between the public perception of the church body and the stories told to the pastoral staff. For the sin to stop, it cannot be hidden. It's our pride as a church body that hides the sin and protects the sinner. Confidentiality is a big thing, and I get that. Pastors can't get up in front of the church and start the service by revealing their congregants' private matters. But the pastor can preach on those topics. While preaching verse by verse through Scripture reveals some wonderful things, pastors also need to address the things the church won't discuss. And one of those things is domestic violence.

Screening Pastors and Staff for Domestic Violence

When it comes to church staff and leadership, what checks, screenings, or personal evaluations are employed to ensure domestic violence isn't present in their homes? When interviewing or recruiting pastors and staff, what questions are asked? What home studies are conducted? What procedures are followed to try to ascertain if there's domestic violence, and what sort(s), if any, are present? Are there any follow-up interviews one, two, five, or ten years down the road to check on the family's well-being and determine if abuse has crept into the family? What services are available to church staff and leadership if these evaluations reveal domestic violence?

I can hear people grumbling, "What goes on in my home ain't nobody else's business." Really? Can a man who abuses his wife and family lead sheep to the gates of heaven? The Bible says church leaders are held to a higher standard, and any accusations should be dealt with publicly as a deterrent to other arrogant leaders who think they can get away with domestic violence. Yes, deal with it publicly. If addressed privately, the abuse could continue unabated until criminal charges could finally be filed after decades of pedophilia, child abuse, and domestic violence.

How Do We Move Forward?

What's the first step? How do we move forward? First, church leadership—from the very top—needs to agree that domestic violence is an issue inside the church. Then there must be education about domestic violence from the kindergarteners to the most tenured seminary professors, from Sunday school through the head pastors, and from small group Bible studies to conferences, seminars, and workshops. Equally important, we must be willing to believe, support, help, and protect the women, children, and men who are being abused among us. We are the hands and feet of Christ to those who are vulnerable and hurting—but not if we do nothing. It's time for us to do something.

Church leadership—from the very top—needs to agree that domestic violence is, indeed, an issue inside the church.

Furthermore, we need curriculum packages designed to teach children of all ages the key components of good relationships, how to identify what leads to bad relationships, and how to evaluate the relationships one is in. Train children to identify problems with questions such as:

- What do we do when we see good components in others or ourselves?
- What do we do when we see bad components?
- How do we handle these things in social settings?
- How do we protect ourselves and others from things that lead to unhealthy relationships?
- How do we identify if we are in unhealthy relationships, and what do we do to keep and maintain healthy relationships?
- How do we defend ourselves or others?
- How do we handle these things publicly and in the privacy of our homes?
- How do we handle these things when the person exhibiting poor relationship choices is bigger, stronger, or more powerful than us?
- How do we handle it when someone else is oppressed by a bigger, stronger, or more powerful person?

You can see that these questions and answers apply to so much more than domestic violence. A good foundation about how to arrive at healthy answers to these questions, along with self-defense training, will go a long way toward reducing domestic violence as well as bullying.

One final thought regarding the great love passage from 1 Corinthians 13: Realize that we each read that passage with certain assumptions about what it means. And the abuse victim has distorted assumptions. When it says we need to believe all things, victims of abuse think that means we need to believe our abuser when they tell us they're sorry and will not hurt us again. When it says we need to always trust, that means we must always trust our abuser. When it says love endures all things, that means we need to endure the abuse quietly and stoically, just as Christ did on the cross.

These assumptions need to be tossed. When we live with an abuser, we know what our abuser is. We know they're vindictive and vengeful. We know they lie. We know they're controlling, jealous, or manipulative. We know they hurt us all the time. When the passage says love trusts, I don't think it means we must lie to ourselves and convince ourselves that God wants us to trust a liar. We need to trust what we know is the truth. We need to trust that the person we know is a liar and is going to lie. We need to endure not through endless abuse but through the repercussions of it—when we set the boundaries to keep ourselves safe and the children safe and when we say no, no more. And when we plan to begin life away from the abusive relationship, we need to endure a lot. That's what this passage says.

> *We need to trust what we know is the truth.*

We must continue our godly, God-fearing behavior despite what our abuser does. This requires some thought. It's a different perspective that requires discernment and wisdom to apply this passage to your situation. But I guarantee you, when it says we need to believe all things, it doesn't mean when your husband tells you you're a good-for-nothing b%&^*#, you need to believe it. You need to believe that your husband is abusive, and you need to take steps to stop the abuse. Don't tell yourself it's not possible. Tell yourself the truth and believe the truth. Remember, the truth will set you free.

It's not enough to look around our beloved congregation and say that everybody looks great; we don't have domestic violence in our church. No. It's right under our noses. We must acknowledge its presence and deal with it in a manner suitable for the Christian name we bear. Is God happy when we hide it, ignore it, and blame the victim? Does God approve when we tell the victim, as in James 2:16, "Go in peace, be warm and well fed," and do nothing about their physical needs? We have a collective and individual responsibility to live out true religion and to visit widows and orphans in their affliction.

PART 5

Escape and Recovery from Domestic Violence

13

Options/Safety Planning

Assuming that this book has become more personal than you ever thought it would be, there are many, many, many decisions and plans to make to protect yourself and your children and start on the road to healing. It's daunting and overwhelming. It's scary. You're already dealing with so much, and now, you must add more preparation and planning than you can imagine. But it's critical to your survival, empowerment, and children. You can do this. You must.

Next, we'll look at the following to be sure you're making the best decisions for yourself and your children and are prepared to follow through:

1. Option 1: Stay as you are
2. Option 2: Stay in the marriage and fight from within
3. Option 3: Separate or divorce
4. Option 4: Creativity
5. Financial planning
6. Safe exit planning
7. Shelter planning

8. Childcare planning
9. Planning for necessities
10. Planning for retaliation/vengeance
11. Legal counsel, aid, and protective orders
12. Evidence collection
13. Emotional preparation/ability to remove emotions
14. DV counselors

This chapter deals with the nuts and bolts of what you need to consider. For those who hear about domestic violence and wonder why anyone would stay in that situation, this chapter will give insight into why it's so much easier to suggest that the victim leave than it is to do so. The bottom line is that it's hard to leave because it's *dangerous*.

The most difficult thing you may handle is your feelings as a mother. Every single mother I have talked to, heard about, and read about will do absolutely anything to keep her children with her. We're afraid of losing our children. We cannot bear the thought of them being apart from us forever. Your abuser knows this. So does your abuser's attorney. And they'll use this knowledge to negotiate in their favor and to you and your children's detriment. Be aware of this and try to think of ways to leverage your love for them in your favor instead of theirs. Think. They'll threaten you with taking away the children to get you to cave on things that are important to them. They'll pretend to be devoted to the children to keep them from you for however long they can get. Be ready for that.

So how can you turn that around? How can you use their lack of interest or responsibility for the children in your favor? Have examples of things, issues, and testimony that demonstrate they're lying about how much they care. Be ready to present that at a moment's notice.

When I was trying to divorce, my husband's attorney said that my husband wanted to retain control of the money and give me an allowance for food for the children and me. There was no way I was going to agree with that. He'd already demonstrated that he would withhold the money we needed to survive. The judge seemed to think his attorney's request was reasonable and turned to me for my opinion. Whenever I tried to respond with more than a yes or no answer, I was interrupted and cut off. So instead, I said, "Considering my husband has let my vehicle insurance expire, and the children's medical bills go to collections, I'm not sure I can trust him to handle the money responsibly." The judge stared at me for a moment. Then he said, "Well, we aren't in a trial right now, so strike that from the record." But at least it was said and heard.

Now, let's talk about your options for going forward.

Option I: Stay as You Are

If you're reading this and realize that your marriage is abusive, you have some decisions to make. First, congratulations on taking the fundamental first step to recognize your situation. There will undoubtedly be readers who recognize their position and will deny it and fight against the truth.

On numerous occasions, someone posted a message on a Christian homeschool, marriage, or Facebook page that held the same despair and desperation I used to feel. Stories that triggered me because they were so similar to mine. Knowing their pain, I'd respond and suggest they check out the meaning of domestic violence. And many times, I'd be slammed with angry and vehement defenses about how much their husband loved them and what a wonderful man he was, and

If you're reading this and realize that your marriage is abusive, you have some decisions to make.

how dare I suggest that their beloved husband was violent with her or the children.

That's OK. If that's you, it's OK. I fought against that knowledge for twenty-five years before realizing the truth. There may never come a time when your mind will stop fighting it. And that's OK, too.

This book is borne of my experience, journey, and education in domestic violence. It's highly personal to me and may not affect you or your thoughts or life. And that's OK. But if this book has opened your eyes to some truths in your life, congratulations on seeing them and starting the process of accepting what was once an unmentionable reality.

Your first option is to continue as you were before you read this. Just keep on keepin' on. Out of denial of the truth, or deliberate choice to continue accepting the abuse, you have that option—to stay in it. Just realize that abuse doesn't improve but escalates over time, and every minute you choose to remain in an abusive situation is one more minute of teaching your children that abusive relationships are the way of life. Every minute you stay brings the children one minute closer to being doomed to repeat your situation. You can choose to stay. And your children will learn from that. If you choose to stay, I strongly recommend educating yourself about domestic violence and seeing a counselor who can help you deal with it in healthy ways.

Option 2: Stay in The Marriage and Fight from Within

The second option is where I ended up—staying and fighting from the inside. This option is terrifying and extremely difficult (not that any of the choices are easy). But this is the one I know best, and it's really hard. It's hard for several reasons:

- There's an established pattern that exists in your marital relationship. It was probably there before you even married in how you interact, the assumptions you've both made about each other, the words you both choose and your attitudes. There are patterns of behavior and sequences of events that are thoroughly ingrained. When he says or does x, you say or do y. All that must change. Not only does it have to change, but you also must learn what things *you* have to change. It takes a lot of effort and mind control to deliberately stop your autopilot behavior and responses to go in a different direction. It's hard to break those patterns and frightening because you don't know how your abuser will react until the moment is upon you. It takes great bravery and courage.
- You may be working on changing as hard as possible, but your abuser wants things to stay the same. So, while you're working in one direction, your abuser is pulling as hard as possible in the other. It's tremendously exhausting and frustrating. Your abuser is counting on that, and he's counting on wearing you down, so you'll go back to how things were. For me, going back to how things were has sometimes been mighty tempting. Even though it's so painful, sad, depressing, and miserable, it would be easier psychologically. You must continually guard against this temptation. You must keep your long-term objective in mind—freedom for yourself and your children from the curse of abuse that's being passed down to another generation. And you may wind up saving your lives as well.
- It's hard to realize that things you did and do to cope or deal with the abuse—or even out of ignorance about what was happening—are exactly what your abuser counts on to keep the abuse cycle going. In a

bizarre way, our actions contribute to the cycle. This is devastating to recognize. It's also one of the keys to opening the door to freedom. As I look back, I'm horrified about things I did or didn't do, thinking at the time that it was the right thing or that it was innocent. I feel guilty about what my children suffered because I was ignorant about domestic violence and the part I was playing in it. But now I know. And now you can know, too, which means you can do something about it. You can recognize when you're falling into a pattern, and you can stop and change it. Don't let regret or guilt dominate your thoughts. If you recognize something that made things worse for you or your children, talk to your kids, apologize, and tell them you'll be changing things. Ask for their help. If you know that you behave a particular way in certain situations and you want to change it, ask the children to help you see it. Invite them to talk about things and share their feelings and perceptions. Open up discussions. That's how change and healing begin.

Option 3: Separate or Divorce

This option requires a good deal of money and a willingness to abide by the court's decisions, regardless of your personal feelings about those decisions. If children are involved, unless your abuser is going to prison, there will be custody and visitation issues, meaning you'll most likely still be in contact with your abuser.

Interestingly, when I filed for divorce and decided I was not willing to abide by what the court would rule, I dropped the case. As soon as I dropped it, life at home became much worse. But now, after having the mediator involved, my husband is out of the home, and we're finally safe, secure, and generally happy. It's worked out much better than I could have ever hoped for.

As a Christian, I credit God with bringing this all about. However, due to my experiences, I firmly believe that having a mediator involved who the abuser knows and respects is a critical component to controlling his abusive behaviors. If there are people in your sphere of influence who know both you and your abuser, and there's a person who can clearly see and address abusive behaviors while retaining the respect of your abuser, pray about asking this person to become an unbiased third party.

But it's risky, risky, risky, risky. You may be inviting more abuse. You must be certain that person understands abuse, its ramifications, and all its issues. Mr. Nice Guy or Ms. Had-Some-Counseling-Classes will be unable to help you, and he or she may even make it worse. But it has been an absolute Godsend in my situation.

The other thing about going with the court's orders is that, as a victim of domestic violence, we're conditioned to believe that abuse, lies, manipulations, and unconscionable behavior toward us is what we should expect and experience, and we must obey anything and everything perfectly and happily. When we have court orders, we feel we must do everything ordered or go to jail. But our abuser has no such compulsion. They'll disregard orders, try to compel you to make exceptions, and try to work your pity and compassion to excuse their disobedience because of various excuses. Then if you bend the rules for them, they'll address that in court and say you aren't abiding by the order.

A young woman I know experienced this exact thing. Because of the abuse, I helped to completely move her, her children, and their possessions out of the house he was supposed to be paying for. She got a restraining order and court orders regarding visitation and how the transfer of children was to occur. I was there when he called to say he couldn't come at the prescribed time and asked if she would meet him later. There were a couple of problems with this:

1. Contacting her this way violated the restraining order.
2. Asking for a change violated the court-ordered terms of transfer.

The woman explained that she couldn't agree to meet him later because she had to leave for work and the children needed to be with him before she could go. He whined and begged and excused until, finally, she agreed. Of course, she was late for work.

He then made a recording that accused this young woman of violating the restraining order and the terms of transfer because she didn't deliver the children at the prescribed time and place—even though he had badgered her into changing everything! None of these violations were reported. Violations continued. Regrettably, the couple is back together again at the time of this writing.

When you separate or initiate a divorce, the mind games will escalate; you can be sure of that. One benefit to using the courts where I live is that there's a protocol for communication that must go through the court system. If the abuser is supposed to have custody from 5:00 p.m. on Friday to 10:00 a.m. on Sunday, and he wants to pick up the kids at 7:30 p.m. because he has to work late, instead of calling you and harassing you about it, he has to go through the court communication system. That reduces the chances that he'll create chaos in the schedule just to rattle you because the court will have it on record that he initiated a request to disobey

When you separate or initiate a divorce, the mind games will escalate; you can be sure of that.

the court order. That makes him look bad. If there's no court communication system, then do your best to always have a third party in on the conversation.

Option 4: Creativity

Your fourth option is to do anything that works that's different from the above three options. Here are some things that my experience has shown to be important:

- Have no contact. Some situations will make this impossible. But whenever possible, eliminate all contact with your abuser.
- When contact is necessary, always, always, always have a third party in on the communication as a witness, and any changes must *always* be in writing with more than one copy. This is a bother, wastes time, and is highly aggravating, but it is absolutely necessary. When the abuser's words can be used against him, you win every time. Just remember that what you say can be used against you also, which leads to the next point.
- Keep yourself above reproach. There can be nothing that your abuser can use to accuse you. That means no angry outbursts or swearing at him. No trying to trick him, set him up, or disobeying laws. I belong to a Facebook group called Overcoming Narcissistic Abuse. Sometimes, people put up screenshots of text conversations between them and their abuser. Then they say stuff about how abusive their abuser is. But there's so much profanity from both sides that I can't tell who's the abuser and who's the victim. They both sound equally abusive to me. This is what you must guard against. You must be beyond reproach in everything.

You cannot follow your abuser around and take pictures. You cannot spy or eavesdrop or stalk. You cannot yell or scream or slander the abuser to all their friends and acquaintances. You must carry on with your life and mind your business, but at the same time, be very prepared so that if your abuser yells or screams or is profane; if your abuser tricks you, sets you up, or disobeys laws; if your abuser follows you around and takes pictures; if your abuser spies or eavesdrops or stalks, then *you must make record of it* in every way available to you and keep it as evidence to be used in court to prove your case.

Remember that the courts are far more concerned with the abuser's rights to be presumed innocent and his or her rights to access the children than whether your claims are true. So regardless of which path you choose, you must have clearly demonstratable evidence and an enormous, overwhelming amount of it for the courts to consider that you might be right in your assessment of the abuse. Document everything, all the time, every time.

Start documenting from the second you think you might be in an abusive relationship. The church will probably come against you for this because, by their standard, that's "keeping a record of wrongs," which 1 Corinthians 13 tells us not to do. But it's important to document for the courts, so do it anyway.

Document everything, all the time, every time.

But even further, it's important to document what happens and what's said for your mind and your sanity. Countless times, I had conversations with my husband about hundreds of things. I understood what I thought he said and meant and would proceed accordingly, only to have him later say that no, he never said any such thing. Since it was a verbal conversation, I had no proof, but I knew inside that what he now said wasn't true. Sometimes, I just chalked it up to forgetting, but it happened so often. And many times, the things were opposite of what I remembered. Or he would say that I said those things myself, not him, or I felt this way or that way, not him. This is lying, deception, gaslighting, projection, and crazymaking, and it's a favorite tactic of abusers. If you document, you can prove that you're not crazy.

Another reason to keep good documentation is that your memory tends to forget details, situations, extenuating circumstances, and even whole events. So, when things happen, make sure you write them down. If your abuser comes back later with a different version of events, you can demonstrate that he isn't portraying the situation correctly.

If you continually demonstrate that your abuser consistently portrays situations or conversations incorrectly, he'll likely get upset about it. And it will be wearing on you and terribly exhausting. Your abuser will count on your exhaustion and try to wear you down. Your abuser will rely on you to back down if they get upset. You must retain your composure.

There was a time after the mediator got involved when my husband lied to our mediator about a situation on our farm. The children and I used the tractor frequently. My husband, knowing that, deliberately sabotaged it so it wouldn't run. Months passed, and the children and I had to labor by hand to do the work the tractor could have easily done. I finally asked a neighbor to help us fix the tractor. He came over and worked on the electrical harness. My husband, at some later time, took apart what the neighbor had done so it was inoperable again. The next time my neighbor came over, he was mad as a hornet that his electrical work had been taken apart. He re-did it for us because he knew what my husband was up to.

Quite some time later, when talking about how my husband would sabotage my efforts, I mentioned the tractor to our mediator. My husband insisted that our neighbor worked on the carburetor, not the electrical harness. I refused to accept that and called my neighbor to back me up. Unfortunately, he didn't answer the phone, but after we met with our mediator, my husband went to that neighbor's house, waited for him, and told the neighbor that he hadn't worked on the electrical harness; he'd worked on the carburetor, right? Didn't he remember that he worked on the carburetor? Because that's what he did; he worked on the carburetor, not the electrical harness. Unbelievable. Just incredible. It was an incredibly stupid move, illustrative of the fact that abusers will lie even when it does not benefit them. This neighbor was an ex-con and had been in prison for over nine years for attempted murder. And my husband went over there and called him a liar.

No, I wasn't afraid of my neighbor. He was one of the few people who immediately saw through my husband and disliked him from the time they first met. As time went by and we became better friends, he told me his story, and I told him about what we were experiencing and that I was learning I was in an abusive relationship. He and his wife let me know they had my back and would do anything in their power to help me and the children if we needed it. I trusted him more than I trusted my husband.

One night, my daughter was out milking the cows very late. It was somewhere around 11:30 p.m. or midnight. My daughter was livid with the cows for some reason and was screaming at them. I was in the kitchen, oblivious, doing dishes and waiting for the milk to come in, when my phone rang. It was my neighbor.

"I heard you guys screaming," he said. "I'm out by your shop, hiding in the woods. Just come out of the house, and I'll shoot him."

"Nobody screamed," I said, somewhat taken aback. "We're all OK, really."

"I know you're saying that because he's standing right there," he replied. "We heard you guys screaming. So just come out on the porch, and I'll shoot him. Just come outside."

By this time, my daughter got back in the house. I asked if she had yelled at the cows. She started telling me all about it, so I repeated to the neighbor, "We are all OK, really. It wasn't my husband. My daughter was yelling at the cows. All of us are fine. Nothing is going on. I'm so sorry to have disturbed you guys."

After a few more minutes, I finally convinced him to go back home, but he never believed that I was telling the truth, and he was prepared to shoot my husband to protect the children and me.

Facts, Not Feelings

If your abuser realizes that your documentation is an effort to hold him accountable, he'll probably accuse you of ulterior motives—of keeping records of wrongs; of not loving him like you're supposed to; of being suspicious; of being untrustworthy. He may create false documentation to counteract what you're doing. My friend, if these things start happening, you need to understand the truth that your mate, your husband, your soulmate, the person you love, is, in fact, an abusive person. He does not love you; he loves to abuse you. You must come to that realization without emotion and act in your best interests and the best interests of your children.

He does not love you; he loves to abuse you.

This brings us to question what love *is*, Biblically, in a domestic violence situation. There are two things to remember:

1. The ultimate purpose of our lives is to make sure everyone we're connected with does not doubt that we love the Lord, and they're so encouraged by that example

that they're inspired to join us and be with the Lord in Heaven someday. The salvation of souls—that's the objective.
2. The Bible speaks about loving others. Matthew and Mark quote Jesus as clearly discussing this very topic. "Love the Lord your God with all your heart and with all your soul and with all your mind and with all your strength. The second is this: Love your neighbor as yourself. There is no commandment greater than these."

Knowing these two things is critically important when anyone in the church tells you not to keep a record of wrongs. Let's say you have a son. And your son goes to school every day and does dumb things: He cuts the hair of the girls sitting in front of him in class. He lights his schoolbooks on fire under the desk. He steals from the teacher's desk during recess. He clogs up the bathroom toilets.

We would all agree these are problem behaviors. What should happen? Should you pretend he never did any of those things because you "love" him? Will that help him stop the behavior? Should you treat each new infraction like he'd never committed any infractions before? What about the danger to the other students? Should all of that be ignored because you "love" him?

It's clear that the discipline and consequences of those behaviors aren't because you *don't* love him but because you *do* love him. You want him to be a law-abiding citizen and a productive member of society. You want him to grow up to be responsible, considerate of others, empathetic, and kind. You want him to choose to do right, not wrong. You want him to be saved.

In like manner, when someone's abusive, their abuse causes great harm to several people—primarily you. It causes loss of time and money, emotional strain and duress, and physical and mental harm. By not recording these things, are you loving them? Or are you helping them along the path of destruction to the eternal harm of their soul? As time goes on and abusive behaviors become cemented in your children's minds, are you not ensuring that future generations will suffer because you didn't hold your abuser to account?

Loving your partner means holding them to account. In my experience, holding my husband accountable wasn't about making accusations or telling him how bad he was. Holding him accountable meant that I documented everything and used that documentation to keep his lies and other abuses from being used against me and the children.

Perhaps even more importantly, how does protecting your abuser show love to your children? Are your children less worthy of love than your abuser? In a court of law, if someone protects a criminal, they're considered an accomplice or an accessory to the crime. When I fully understood this, I could finally separate all emotion from my dealings with my husband. If I didn't protect my children from him, I would be just as guilty of abuse as he was.

What does it mean to love your neighbor as yourself? Generally speaking, our basic instinct is to take care of ourselves. We eat and drink, and we practice basic hygiene. We keep warm in the winter and cool in the summer. We do the things we need to do to take care of ourselves. The verse asserts that we should take care of other people just like we take care of ourselves, but caring for ourselves is assumed to be our priority. We take care of ourselves first, and then we take care of others. We love ourselves first, and then we love others as we love ourselves.

When we allow ourselves to be abused, we love our abusive partner first and put ourselves last. That reverses the order, and it has consequences. When your partner loves you and puts you first, the love grows. You both are grateful for the love of the other, which makes you want to demonstrate your love and respect for him that much more. But when your partner does not love you or put you first like you do him, you get sucked dry, and there's nothing left for you. You suffer emotionally, mentally, physically, and spiritually. You start to believe that you aren't enough. You are not good enough. You are not worthy of love or acceptance. You have no worth or value.

But the opposite is true. You *are* worthy. You *do* have value. Your value doesn't come because of the love placed on you by others. You have value and worth because you exist because you are created for a purpose and because God loves you. It's critical that *you love yourself first* and then love your partner. When you reverse the order, bad things happen. Take care of yourself first.

Leaving the Relationship

You must have a plan to keep you and your children safe if you decide to leave. Don't try to do this alone. Talk to everyone you can think of—crime victim advocates, women's advocates, domestic violence shelter personnel, counselors, lawyers, etc. Think of everything you might need to leave the relationship behind. Use the following worksheet or make up your own that is more suitable for you. Inevitably, I will not have thought of everything, so think about it and add to this list.

Try to anticipate things your abuser may do to exact vengeance: destroying your vehicle, smashing out windows, kicking in doors, bashing holes in the walls, trying to take the children, locking you out of financial accounts, hacking into your social media, email, or phone accounts, removing you from the phone plan, removing your car from the insurance policy, threatening your relatives, stealing or killing or injuring your pets, destroying heirlooms or sentimental possessions, changing the locks on the house. They'll do anything and everything to lash out.

The most dangerous time for you is when you leave the relationship. So, plan it out thoroughly, take action, and don't look back. If you're a Christian woman and believe the standard doctrinal presentation that God hates divorce, please know that I'm not advocating for divorce or saying that divorce is your only option. I'm not divorced, although I plan to be eventually. There are an infinite number of ways this can all play out. But in the meantime, you must keep yourself and the children safe. You must leave the abuse. Then you can deal with what will happen going forward. But first, the abuse must stop, and the best way to stop it is to get away from your abuser.

The following checklist is a starting point to get you thinking:

ITEM	Secured Yes/No	NOTES
Emergency clothing for everyone that's easily accessible		
Emergency medicines/toiletries for everyone that are easily accessible		
Valuables stored safely (jewelry, sentimental items, policies/contracts, bank/investment/retirement account information, etc.)		
Titles with your name on them (vehicles, real estate, equipment, etc.) acquired and stored safely		
Pets' lodging and care arranged for		
Emergency contacts are easily accessible in case you need them		

ITEM	Secured Yes/No	NOTES
All important information from your phone or device is backed up to something else or printed out in case your phone is destroyed		
Speak with an attorney about moving children and changing pickup legal forms		
Where you will stay secured		
Speak to an attorney about documenting/recording/videotaping etc., your abuser without their knowledge		
A job or form of income secured		
Notify schools/daycare/athletic teams and change paperwork so the abuser cannot pick up.		
Obtain an Order of Protection if necessary		
Women's or Victim's advocate contacted for available resources		
All available resources contacted for aid		
All passwords/security codes changed, or get new devices/accounts entirely		
Create bank accounts in your name only, and put any money you can legally obtain in those accounts.		
Schedule your safe exit, or know your plan if an emergency exit becomes necessary		
Exit Day		

Financial Planning

To take care of yourself and the children, you must begin planning. The first thing you're going to need is money. If you're a stay-at-home mom, maybe there's some work you can do from home. You can sell homemade crafts, décor, knitting/crocheting projects, jewelry, soaps, etc., on Etsy, Facebook Marketplace, and eBay. If you're trained in a skill like accounting or writing, you may be able to find a work-from-home job. If your children are old enough or go to school full time, you may be able to get a part-time job. If none of those things are possible because of a disability, financial abuse, or something else, you'll need to tighten your belt and scrape out little bits from what you're given whenever you can.

Start a bank account in your name for when you get a little bit of cash. Start thinking about a budget. What kind of income will you need to pay for necessities if your partner contributes nothing? Dave Ramsey's Financial Peace class is great, but it costs money. If you can't afford to take a class, figure out what you spend each month and for what. If you're going to move out, find out what a suitable place costs and put the rent cost in your budget. Here are some other costs to include in your budget:

- Water
- Sewer
- Electric
- Trash
- Gas or propane
- Food for you and the kids (if you have any)
- Car insurance and gas
- Phone and internet

There are a lot of ways you can save money. Only shop at thrift stores, don't eat out, shop at the cheapest grocery store and be happy with off-brands and clearance sales. Just flat out make do with less. Penny pinching is critically important. Put everything you possibly can into your personal account. Save, save, save, save. Figure out what you must do to get the monthly income you'll need when you leave, and start doing it now.

I was a stay-at-home mom. I'd owned my own interior decorating business at one time. When I was in my fifth pregnancy, I tried to turn it into a strictly online business, so I wouldn't have to go to appointments anymore and the business wouldn't be limited to my local area. Anybody, anywhere could find it and order window treatments, bedding, etc.

My husband was a tech person, but I'm not, so I created the website, made fabric selections, ordering menus, tutorials, and everything. But I didn't know how to set up the shopping cart and the payment acceptance procedures. I needed his help. But he wouldn't help me. Several years later, he told me he purposely sabotaged my business so I wouldn't have my own income.

After my fifth child was born, I shut down my business and was a full-time mom. We began homeschooling the following year, so the children and I were always home and together. We worked, did chores and projects, did school, played, read books, went on field trips, volunteered to help people, cared for each other, argued, and did all the normal things families do. And I was completely dependent on my husband and his income.

As long as I believed he loved me and was doing what was best for us, I didn't care. But that changed once I realized our situation—that not only did he not love us, but he was certainly not doing what was best for us. Once I realized I was fully dependent on him and he, in his mind, was under no

IS THIS DOMESTIC ABUSE?

obligation to do anything to benefit us, I saw that my situation was desperate. I had no money or income or way to earn an income. The last time I'd been employed was twenty-plus years ago, before I got married. I had eight children still at home; the youngest was only five. We homeschooled, and I wasn't willing to put my children in a public school.

I was truly stuck. I was under his thumb. I knew it, and I knew he knew it because as soon as I tried to get out from under him, he transferred all the money into his personal account and left me with $8.32 in the account. When I asked him how I was supposed to feed our children on $8.32, he said I should have figured that out before, and it was not his problem.

If you can start earning an income on your own in any way, do it, and do it now. Figure out whatever you must for the kids' school, childcare, etc., and try to get something for a few hours a week while your abuser is normally gone. Open an account in your name alone, so your abuser can't see what's in there or where it's coming from. Save every dime for the upcoming emergency. Learn now how to be as frugal as you possibly can. Find the cheapest stores, so you save on clothing and household needs. Start stockpiling some staples and keep them hidden in your safe place: diapers and wipes, blankets and bedding, kitchen things, toiletries, non-perishable food items, etc. If your marriage is salvaged and you don't need those things, you can always bring them home and use them or donate them to another mom in dire straits.

> *If you can start earning an income on your own in any way, do it, and do it now.*

Know that as believers, God does not forget about us. We may be in an awful situation, but that doesn't mean God is causing it or that He isn't there. He certainly proved that to me.

The children and I had worked at a farmer's market for a couple of years and became friends with one of the farmers. We volunteered to help him on his farm for several years. Coincidentally, the year I realized how bad our situation was, our farmer friend had tremendous bumper crops. He dropped off enormous barrels and boxes of tomatoes, peppers, sweet corn, and other produce every week. We canned all summer long—hundreds of jars of pickles, tomatoes, salsas, and jams and dozens of bags of frozen corn, beans, and beets. In November of that year, my husband left only $8.32 in the account for me to buy groceries. But our farmer friend had been so generous all summer that we had plenty. God provided for us through our friend all year long, and we had enough to eat well, even when my husband tried to punish us financially. Three years later, we were still eating those canned tomatoes!

Safe Exit Planning

It's critical to have a safe exit strategy. You cannot be over-prepared. You alone need to do this. Nobody can help you because every situation is unique. Think about the following:

- What situations would make it necessary for me to leave on very short notice?
- If that should happen, what would I need to take with me?
- How will I get the children and all necessities out with me?
- Where will I go?
- How will I make sure nothing important is damaged or destroyed?
- Where are all important documents, like birth certificates, vehicle titles, insurance papers, etc.?

IS THIS DOMESTIC ABUSE?

- Who can I call on to help in an emergency?
- Would my departure put anyone at risk?
- What can be done to minimize any risks?
- Are there any guns in the house?
- Where are they, and if the abuser heads in that direction, how much time will you have to get out?

Other Suggestions:

- It might be a good idea to practice drills with the children and time how fast you can all get outside and into the car.
- It might be a good idea to have some things in place already. Store important documents, including your will, at a trusted person's home.
- Have a backpack for each child filled with necessities in the trunk of the car.
- Have a pre-existing agreement with someone that, in case of an emergency, you can stay with them for a while in their home.
- Consider getting a prepaid cell phone like a Tracphone or something similar, so your abuser can't track you or hack into your email or text messages.
- Change passwords on social media accounts, email accounts, etc., so you can't be stalked online.
- Make a list of potential places where you might be able to get a quick, entry-level job, like gas stations, fast food places, retail stores, grocery stores, temporary agencies, etc. Preferably somewhere your abuser is not likely to go.
- Make sure any paychecks are auto-deposited into your personal account.

Shelter Planning

You're going to need a roof over your head. Consider a women's shelter, a hotel room, a bedroom at your parent's house, or a good friend's home. These will be helpful in the short term, but they're all temporary, for emergency purposes only. You cannot overstay your welcome with family or friends or stay longer than a certain length of time at shelters. A hotel will get very expensive very quickly. So immediate, emergency housing is good but only for a limited time.

You must figure out where to live for the long haul. Here's the thing. If you leave because of an abusive incident and go back for any reason at all, it implies several things to your abuser:

- You're emotionally unable to leave the relationship. You "love" your abuser too much, or your abuser is just so awesome that you cannot live without them. This allows the abuser to gain more power. If you actually can't live without them, there's nothing they cannot do to you. You're giving them a free license to kill you and your children. Whatever your reason, your abuser will only believe that the "real" reason you came back was because you cannot live without them.
- In a practical sense, you cannot leave the relationship because of money, housing, and providing for your necessities. Whatever it is, you can't do it alone. Again, this gives the abuser great power. He knows that you are 100 percent dependent upon his goodwill. You are now dirt to be ground under his foot.
- The first two implications confirm to your abuser's mind that you are, indeed, worthless and stupid. The only thing that makes you worth anything is because you're with him. Therefore, he'll make sure you know

that. Statistics show that women generally leave and return to an abusive relationship seven times before leaving for good. Don't do that to yourself and the children. Make your plans. And when you decide it's time to leave, leave! Execute your plans and move forward.

Leaving for a short time won't make him desperate for you to return. He may talk like he is, but those are just more lies. If you go back, he'll despise you for continuing to accept the treatment that he knows is awful. If you can take that and still go back to him, things will just get worse.

My advice is to get yourself and your children as ready as possible, and when the time comes for you to leave, don't go back. Do whatever you have to do to stay away. That's your first demonstration that you aren't stupid or worthless. You don't need him to survive, nor do you even want him. This will be a blow to his ego. He'll be waiting for you to come crawling back, longing for his awesomeness. When you don't, you become a threat to his control. That's why leaving is the most dangerous time. That's why planning is so important.

If you decide to make the break, consider whether you need a restraining order. Do what you can to keep your location unknown to him or others who would tell him where you are. If you're afraid of retribution, anticipate what he could or would do and take steps to circumvent it. Preparation is key. Think of as many details as you can and do what you can to prepare ahead of time. Remember to document everything in every way you can think of.

Fooling Ourselves

We never want to think of our abusers as people who mean to hurt us. We like to make excuses for them in our minds.

They aren't good at communicating. They're bipolar. They're stressed. They had a bad day. They just don't realize how hurtful they are. They have an anger management issue. They just don't understand children. They grew up in an abusive home, and they don't know how to not be abusive and on and on and on. We like to tell ourselves what we're living with is not that bad, especially if he isn't physically abusive. Other people die! Our partner is really a good person; they just . . . whatever. He would never do anything that would seriously hurt us. Underneath it all, he loves me; he just doesn't know how to show it.

Did you know that 58 percent of female homicides are committed by their partner? Fifty-eight percent of the women killed are killed by their husbands or boyfriends. *Fifty-eight percent!* Just because your partner has not killed you yet doesn't mean he's incapable of it. Especially if there's a firearm in the house. Fatality goes up by 500 percent when a gun is in the home.

Childcare planning

Planning for the care of your children will be tricky. Parents, relatives, or nearby friends may be able to help you temporarily during the immediate crisis. But eventually, you'll need to pay for it or trade for it. Don't be afraid to try bartering. Could you trade cleaning or landscaping services at a church in exchange for daycare in their preschool? Maybe trade some service you can offer an individual for babysitting. Maybe find an immigrant to babysit and offer English classes in exchange. Think outside the box. The more creative you are, the better. Could you find work during the day while your children are in school? As your children get older, they may be able to handle childcare themselves. I had nine children, and I frequently left them alone because the older ones could supervise the youngsters. If your oldest child or children are mature at twelve or thirteen, they might be responsible enough to help if they get home from school at 4:00 and you have to work until 6:00.

Planning for Necessities

Planning the escape may take some time. It's not something to enter lightly or without preparation. Just keep collecting evidence, keep preparing, and keep saving. Make a plan and stick to it. Then when the time comes, you'll know what you're doing, where to go, how you'll manage, and how you'll keep everyone as safe as possible—and you'll have evidence to give the court so you have the best possible chance of retaining custody of the children if it should come to that.

Investigate food stamps, low-rent housing through the government, food pantries and their requirements, government health clinics for the children, etc. All those assistances are available, but you'll have to familiarize yourself with the requirements, so you'll know if you qualify. Check out local government resources for legal aid, free counseling, rent assistance, utility assistance, etc. If you have young children, WIC (Women, Infants, and Children) may be able to help you. Ask everyone you talk to if other resources are available, like free or reduced legal help, job training or placement, etc. Understand as much as you can before you leave. And remember that no plan will prepare you for every eventuality. The way you plan things out may never happen, but the more you know, the more you'll be able to handle whatever comes to pass.

Things to pack/store away for emergencies:

TOILETRIES

- Toothpaste/brushes for everybody
- Feminine hygiene products for all of-age females
- Hair care products
- Children's bathing supplies
- Infant care products: diaper rash, teething gel, pain reliever/fever reducer, gas relief, cough and cold meds, lotions, and bathing supplies
- Medicines/first aid/prescriptions
- Health and beauty supplies
- Toilet paper/wipes
- Sanitizer
- Paper towels, paper plates, some plastic utensils
- Miscellaneous: insect repellent, allergy meds, pain reliever, vitamins/supplements, etc.

CLOTHING ITEMS

- Baby care: diapers of various sizes, t-shirts, clothes of various sizes and seasons, blankets, socks/footwear
- Children's seasonally appropriate clothing, plus some spare out-of-season clothes
- Your clothes
- Towels/washcloths
- Pillows/blankets/sleeping bags
- Coats, gloves, hats, scarves, warm footwear
- Favorite stuffed animals or blankies

VALUABLES

- Jewelry
- Heirlooms or sentimental items

- Cash or cash equivalents
- Collectibles that are honestly worth something

DOCUMENTS

- Insurance policies
- Deeds for property
- Titles for vehicles
- Will and end-of-life documents
- Documents proving ownership of anything that's yours
- Driver's license, passport, social security cards, and birth certificates for you and all the children

These lists are not comprehensive but will be useful in jogging your memory regarding important things. Write down anything else that's important to you and your children.

Planning for Retaliation/Vengeance

Remember what I said about keeping yourself above reproach? I'm not talking about planning retaliation/vengeance on your abuser. No. You need to plan for your abuser's retaliation/vengeance against you for having the audacity to leave him. In my experience, they're experts at striking in completely unexpected ways.

After I tried to divorce, my husband worked hard to pamper the children and tried to turn them against me. He let them do anything and everything they wanted. He bought them stuff, and he let them play on his computer and watch videos on his iPad—things he had never done or allowed before. When I asked the children to do any chores or do their homework, he generated an attitude of, "It's too bad your mom is such a drag. We could be having fun, except Mom's making you do stuff." I was furious that he manipulated them and tried to turn them against me. It was devastating, terrifying, and incredibly difficult to live with.

I couldn't get angry or confront him because that was what he wanted the children to see. I still needed to be the mother, teach, train, discipline, and ensure their chores and schoolwork got done, which made me the "bad guy." It was astonishing how quickly everything flipped, and he was just the greatest dad ever, wooing them instead of mistreating them, being overly harsh, putting them down, ignoring them, or just plain being mean and abusive.

What made it so seductive was this: all they'd wanted their whole lives was for their dad to love them.

What made it so seductive was this: All they'd wanted their whole lives was for their dad to love them. For him to suddenly act that way meant everything to them, as if all their dreams had come true. I knew he was doing this to get back at me and to manipulate them, but they didn't. They believed him. They thought it was real. You need to be prepared for everything: from suddenly, your abuser is just the greatest thing since sliced bread to your abuser could murder you and your whole family—and everything in between. You can't trust him to be safe.

Legal Counsel, Aid, and Protective Orders

I hired an attorney. My husband also had an attorney. Unbelievably, our church elder (the one who had counseled me for years to yield and bless and honor and respect my husband, to turn the other cheek, who told me not to resolve things with the courts but in the church and had told me I had Biblical grounds to file for divorce) was the one who provided my husband with an attorney. I have no idea if he paid for it or if my husband paid for it. I know that my attorney's fees were over $10,000. I borrowed money from my parents and worked out a payment plan, taking money out of my grocery budget for almost two years to pay it off.

Hiring an attorney will be expensive. Domestic cases are notorious for non-payment, so not all attorneys will accept a case like yours, and if they do, they may require payment upfront. So, your best option may be to investigate local domestic violence resources for free or reduced legal assistance. Talk to local shelters and call the Domestic Violence hotline to see where they can refer you. Always check their requirements to make sure you qualify. I didn't qualify for most programs because my husband earned a good wage. It didn't matter that I couldn't access any of it; since he earned that much, I didn't qualify.

Handling the children is tricky. If you leave with them, your abuser may press kidnapping charges against you. Get counsel about how to protect the children without getting yourself into trouble. Talk to an attorney before you go anywhere or do anything.

Restraining orders or orders of protection may be helpful for you. If there's a history of physical or sexual violence against you, the children, other children, or people, or violence against pets, you're more likely to obtain an order. And even if you do get a court order, you must determine if your abuser will respect the order or if he'll view it as a challenge to defy. If your abuser has and uses a gun, think very hard about what you want to do.

The orders are only useful if you report violations. I have a friend who has an order of protection, and every Friday, her husband comes and walks around the house, looking in the windows, taking pictures, and banging on doors for an hour or so before he leaves. She can't report it because he's supposed to take their two girls on Friday evenings. Except both children are over sixteen, and neither wants to go with him. She isn't going to make the children go with her abuser. But he's following a court order for visitation. So, they hide in a place with no windows every week and stay there until he leaves. When he shows up at other times, she can make a report, and she has. But she felt terrible about it because that meant a warrant was out for his arrest. You must get past that. You cannot feel sorry for the poor abuser, having to suffer some consequences for years of abuse toward you and the children. The abuse must stop, and if it takes an arrest and jail time, praise God! You didn't die!

Evidence Collection

I've said this before, but documentation is *everything*. Courts cannot determine who's telling the truth unless you have proof. The burden of proof is on you, the accuser. Therefore, you must use voice recordings, video recordings, photographs, screenshots of text and email threads, etc. Anything that can be documented, document.

Speak with attorneys first because it may not be legal to record things without your abuser's knowledge. With my patent pending Data Collection System outlined in Chapter 6, when the system is activated on behalf of a victim, messages in all available formats are sent to the abuser telling them the Data Collection System has been activated. Anything they say, do, or communicate in any way, public or private, can and will be used against them in a court of law. But until the app is generally available, you need to know if you're allowed to record information without your abuser's knowledge.

Whatever you're allowed to document, record and document everything you possibly can. Keep it safe, make backup copies, store backups in a safe place away from your home, and have multiple flash drives or wherever you store them. You want a lot of pieces out there, so if your abuser destroys one, they haven't destroyed all your evidence.

Set up your phone's desktop so that camera, audio recording, and notes are on the front, along with anything else you use all the time. Try to find apps that are instant access. Some apps are already out there that are emergency contacts or record events. Check them out and install what will be useful for you. If you don't have a cell phone, you'll always need a camera with you, and you'll always need to know where the nearest phone is. Months may go by between abusive events, or multiple events may happen in a day. The objective is to capture photos, audio or visual recordings, screenshots of social media posts or comments, paper documents you find, text messages, emails, etc.—anything and everything that shows your abuser's nature or the types of abuse you are suffering. Keep a journal to write down anything and everything.

Emotional Distancing

Being emotionally prepared will give you the courage and fortitude to do what needs to be done. Perhaps thinking of something or someone you loved that is now gone may help you understand what I mean. If you had a pet that you loved and it died, that's one of life's most sad times. If a parent, sibling, or child passed away, that was a devastating loss. That's because you're emotionally attached. You love the one who died. But if you read about someone who died in a car crash, you may feel compassion for the survivors, but there's no devastating grief or sense of loss because it wasn't personal. You have no emotional attachment to that person.

Every time your abuser hurts you, you feel grief and loss along the lines of the death of a loved one because your abuser isn't just hurting you; your abuser is killing your hopes and dreams, killing the person you thought you married, killing your marriage and relationship, killing everything about the two of you. You desperately want what you thought you had. Just like you desperately wish a loved person or pet was still alive. Any time your abuser shows any kindness or consideration—brings you a drink, or buys you a candy bar—you so desperately want the person you thought you married to be back that you take that candy bar as a sign that yes, indeed, your beloved is still here. And so, you live your life from one abusive event to the next, looking with all your might for some sign that the partner you thought you had is still alive, enduring abuse after abuse because, you know, deep down, your partner is still in there somewhere.

Every time your abuser hurts you, you feel grief and loss along the lines of the death of a loved one because your abuser isn't just hurting you; your abuser is killing your hopes and dreams.

I get it. I understand. That partner was a fantasy. A vision they created to trick you. That partner is not only dead, but they also never existed. It was all a façade. This is so cruel, so heartless, so horrible. For your sanity and safety going forward, you must grieve the loss of the relationship you thought you had and change your emotional attachment to that of the stranger in the car accident. This abuser is not the person you thought you knew. Your abuser is a stranger. Your love is dead. He or she no longer exists. This person in front of you is a stranger and a dangerous one. You must grieve your loss, for sure, but you also must understand you're dealing with an abusive stranger who will continue to hurt you and the children, and you must keep a clear head, strategize, plan, and escape.

Some of you may say, "With God, all things are possible," which means that abusers can change, even if it seems impossible to us. That's true. But the abuser must *want* it. If your abuser is abusing you, they *do not want to change*. Your abuser will do whatever they must to keep you clinging to hope. They will act repentant, especially in front of other people, so you're pressured not to walk away.

And just because they show signs of repentance, forgiveness doesn't require that you stay in a harmful relationship. Forgiveness means that you have no desire for revenge, no ill will, and leave any judgement or retribution in the Lord's hands. It doesn't mean you need to stay in an abusive relationship. It doesn't mean you must continue to accept abuse. It doesn't mean you have to believe what your abuser says. It certainly doesn't mean you need to keep sleeping with him or living in the same house.

The abuser is a stranger to you, and you must have the same emotional attachment to your abuser as you would have with a stranger. When I realized that unless I stopped the abuse, I was an accomplice, my elder at church told me that I was still married and needed to fulfill my sexual responsibilities to my husband. It almost made me throw up.

"I can't do that," I said, on the verge of puking. "That would be like sleeping with the mailman."

I know that marriage counselors often say that you cannot withhold sex as a means of punishment or to make a point with your partner. But that only applies in relationships that aren't abusive. Sex in an abusive relationship is about control and domination—a tool to be used to gain an end of some kind. The standard marriage counseling advice does not apply in abusive relationships.

DV counselors

Domestic violence counselors are highly personal. They can be amazingly insightful, help you discover all kinds of things you didn't know about yourself, and enable you to adjust your thoughts and behaviors in ways you never imagined. On the other hand, they can be a total bust. Don't give up if you go to one and it's a bust. That simply means your personalities didn't mesh right. Keep trying. You'll find one who works for you.

DV counselors can help you find resources and direct you to other places that offer assistance. They can also help you see what has made you susceptible to abuse and help you to begin changing those things. They can help you identify your behaviors that keep the cycle repeating and help you figure out how you can change your behaviors to break the cycle. They can help you develop a safe exit strategy and give you ideas from countless others who have walked the road before you.

If you cannot find a DV counselor, any counselor specializing in trauma and abuse should work well. But really, the best thing is to find someone who knows their stuff and clicks with you. My counselor specializes in eating disorders and has been wonderful for me. But remember that while you can vent, complain, and cry all hour with your counselor, they can never help you change your abuser. Your job, and your counselor's job, is to see how you can change and break the cycle and start healing. Just take care of yourself. That's the most important thing.

An abusive situation is complicated, stressful, fearsome, anxiety provoking, depressing, and sad. You and your children are allowed—and are worth—a better life filled with love, strength, kindness, compassion, joy, fun, good times, happy holidays, playfulness, and camaraderie. You're worth it. Your children are worth it. So review this chapter repeatedly, make your plan, and execute it.

14

The Children

For survivors with children, things get infinitely more complicated. Not only are you trying to protect yourself and do what's best for you, but you also have several issues with each child. You're concerned about their safety, of course, but you're also concerned about what they think and how they act. What do they consider to be good or not good in a relationship? How do they feel about their relationship with the abuser? Are they also experiencing abuse apart from what's happening to you?

And, of course, there are numerous other necessities: food and clothing, shelter and transportation, school and activities, trauma processing, what they so desperately need in a parent vs. the reality, and how to find other adults to step in to fill in a bit of the gap. It can seem overwhelming. Again, knowledge is power. The more you think, plan, and prepare, the better you can handle issues as they arise—or, better yet, see them coming.

What They See

What *they see* is a big issue, especially because you can't possibly know everything they see, hear, and think about what they see and hear. The only way to know their truth is to ask them, but they won't tell you everything. It's too scary, or they aren't sure what you'll do if you know what they know.

I'm still learning things from my adult children I had no idea about now that they feel safe enough to talk about them. I'm not a child psychologist, nor do I have any idea what the conventional wisdom is about helping children deal with such traumatic issues as abuse. But what I found to be most helpful for myself, and seemingly for them, was to privately address an event in our home with them as soon as we had time alone. Sometimes, that wasn't until the next day or even when the weekend was over. Then I would bring up the event and ask them how they felt. I asked questions about their thoughts and feelings. We would usually end up with the understanding, "Well, we all know that what happened wasn't good for us. I'm working on getting us better. What do you think would help us get better?"

Sometimes, the children brought up things I didn't know about or made suggestions about what we should do in a given situation, but often they didn't say anything. Many times, we had group discussions. Sometimes, they were productive, and sometimes, nobody wanted to talk, but at least it was out in the open.

What They Internalize

This is a much more difficult subject because children often cannot articulate their inner selves. Let's say your abuser hits you and knocks you down, and your child sees that behind a half-open door. You can talk about it later and try to get your child to open up about their feelings. But they won't be able to say things like, "I've learned that I need to hit people when I get mad because that's how I win the argument." They might tell you nothing, that they were scared, or did or didn't like something about the situation, but deep life lessons will most likely be demonstrated later in their behaviors. And it may be a long time later. My adult girls are still wrestling with relationships with men because of what they saw, even though I've been safe from the relationship for a few years now.

Children are often completely unable to articulate their inner selves.

I know that very deep, profound, inexplicable conundrums are internalized. And they are created when words or actions that express love are either followed or preceded by words or actions that are not loving. It's scary for children to know that their life depends on a parent who says and does things that are great on the one hand and horrible on the other—and that no one can predict when what will happen. There's a deep longing for all the great things they know the abuser is capable of as a father or mother, and at the same time, they know they may never experience those great things like other children do. There's tremendous hope every time the abuser says or does something nice—hope that maybe this will last and they'll have the dad or mom of their dreams. And then comes the devastating, dream-crushing reality every time the abuser even "gives them the look."

These highs and lows and massive confusion on a fundamental level set the stage for a whole host of issues: depression and anxiety, self-harm like cutting or hair pulling, teens entering their own dysfunctional romantic relationships, personality disorders, etc. When a parent, upon whom the child's life depends, vacillates between kindness and affection and horrendous violence against the children or the other parent, it harms the child's mental and emotional development. And it lays the groundwork for entering abusive relationships and passing down the expectation of abuse to the next generation.

Manifestations and Symptoms of Trauma from DV

Manifestations are outward signs that DV or abuse could be present, and the child is experiencing it; symptoms indicate that the child is internalizing the patterns of DV, and the child exhibits the behaviors of either the abuser or the victim.

How the child internalizes the abuse somewhat depends on whether the abuser and the victim are his or her parents or if the child is also experiencing abuse. Certainly, some signs considered manifestations of experiencing or witnessing domestic violence may also happen for other reasons, like bedwetting. There are known biological or other reasons for bedwetting, but in my household, bedwetting was one way the trauma of domestic violence manifested in my children. I wasn't certain of this until my husband left our home. My youngest child was eight or nine years old at the time, and three of my youngest children wet the bed almost every night. Within two weeks of my husband leaving, all bedwetting stopped completely without any effort on my part, though we had tried a variety of cures for several years.

How the child internalizes the abuse somewhat depends on whether the abuser and the victim are his or her parents or if the child is also experiencing abuse themself.

Other manifestations of trauma include nightmares, teen promiscuity or very explicit sexual knowledge at an inappropriately young age, cruelty to animals, extreme anger, or anxiety for no apparent reason. Probably the most common manifestations are the relationships the children establish with other children at school or with siblings. If children start exhibiting bully-type behavior, disproportionate aggression, extreme anxiety or depression, inability to concentrate on schoolwork, difficulty maintaining friendships, habitually lying, have precursors to criminal behavior like cheating or stealing from other children in a classroom, etc., DV may be at the root. Again, these things could have other issues at their root. Still, in my experience, children exhibiting these behaviors acted out due to domestic violence or the abuse they'd experienced. If you see these things in your children, have them see a trauma and abuse counselor trained to help them healthily deal with their issues. That would be in addition to solving the domestic violence issues in the home, of course.

Symptoms and manifestations are very similar, but they're not the same. Symptoms can also be manifestations, like cheating or bullying at school. But symptoms can be more than that, and it's prudent to look for subtle things that demonstrate what the children are absorbing. For example, when you tell your child to clean his room, and later you find him playing a game on the computer, and the room is still a disaster, you might say, "I asked you to clean your room. Why are you on the computer when your room is still a mess?" If he says, "I thought you said to clean it tomorrow," he's gaslighting you. If he says, "Well, I knew you were trying to concentrate on something, and I didn't want to disturb you with the noise of the vacuum cleaner," he's being manipulative. If he says, "I did," he's lying. I encourage you to view these things as symptoms that your child is picking up abusive behaviors. Passive aggression, anger, verbal violence, threats, sexually inappropriate interests or actions, deception, and hiding are all symptoms of abusive tendencies, which must be dealt with swiftly and firmly to ensure the child doesn't grow up to be another abuser.

Any behavior that mimics abusive behaviors in any of the categories of abuse shows that the child is absorbing these behaviors. Likewise, behaviors that mimic your responses as a victim show that the child is internalizing behaviors that make them more likely to become victims as adults.

School

If your children go to school (as opposed to homeschooling, daycare, or a preschooler at home), I encourage you to speak to staff. Talk to the school counselor, the principal, and your child's teachers. Tell them what you're learning and ask them to help your child. If your child is experiencing any of the above manifestations, ask the child to see the school counselor regularly or as needed. Ask the teachers to tell you about your child's behavior and be ready to accept it. We can get defensive and excuse poor behavior in our children, but this isn't the time. Now is the time to make sure your child understands good, right, and healthy behaviors, how to identify poor behaviors, and how to make good choices about their behavior. Just because they see bad behavior in an abusive parent doesn't mean it's OK for them to behave poorly at school. There must be consequences to discourage poor behavior patterns from becoming permanently rooted in your child's psyche.

Consider letting your child participate in a sport offered by the school. Not only will this give him or her an outlet for their stress, but it will also give your child a coach who cares for the athletes on the team, provides instruction and mentoring, and acts as a role model. Sometimes, coaches are awful, so go to some games and watch the coaches in action. Talk to the coaches. If it seems like a good fit, find out if your child can join the team. Tell the coach about the situation at home and your child's need for a role model—just so the coach is aware and can reinforce good behavior and be firm on bad behavior. If the coach always yells or swears at the kids, doesn't provide an atmosphere of encouragement, or isn't an honorable role model, look for a different sport or team.

Enlist teachers, coaches, school counselors, etc., to help your children. You don't want them to go easy on your kids. You want them to understand the situation and handle it wisely. They need to know that your child may act out and that you give the adults permission to handle your child with firmness and sensitivity. Your children will need understanding, but they will also need to see how healthy adults act in these situations. A healthy adult sets boundaries and enforces them. A healthy adult understands cause and effect and what that means regarding the choices made. A healthy adult doesn't attack or act out of vengeance or cry and cower down at the slightest provocation. A healthy adult cares, loves, and desires that each child reaches their full potential.

These behaviors are all contrary to what your children have seen in the home. These behaviors will be new, suspect, or perceived as lies by your children, which is why they need help. They need to understand that what they're experiencing at home isn't healthy or good, and they need to learn what *is* healthy and good. That's why the teachers, counselors, and coaches need to know about the DV in your home to become the good and healthy role models your children need.

If your children don't attend school or participate in sporting activities, you must find other men and women who can fill that need. Maybe friends from church, maybe neighborhood families, maybe an elderly couple you can adopt as adoptive grandparents. Seek, and you will find.

Martial Arts

I discovered that martial arts classes were incredible. I took them with my children, and they were so empowering! I cannot overstate how incredible taking these lessons was for all of us. Until I took those classes, I didn't realize how downtrodden I'd become, how low my opinion of myself was, or how much I allowed others to overpower me emotionally, mentally, and physically. Our Sensei (teacher) was focused on the practical application of martial arts in self-defense. Not only did we latch onto it like a drowning person to a life preserver, but we suddenly realized we weren't at the mercy of whoever decided to be mean. We could hold our heads up. We could be confident. We could not be intimidated or hurt by anybody because we knew we could defend ourselves if it came to that. We didn't need to look for a fight, but we didn't have to be afraid there might be one. That removed a huge burden from all of us, especially me.

Shortly after we started taking classes, my husband attacked me. This was outside his normal range of behavior. He was usually abusive with his words and actions, not with a physical attack. We'd started learning about defense from the front and a little bit about defending an attack from the rear but not from the side. Of course, this was the direction the attack came from, and I was not ready. I didn't know what to do, and it paralyzed me. So, I spoke to our Sensei about it. He gave me suggestions, and of course, we kept training. We haven't been able to train for some time, but I still know what I would do. I'm confident that if I was physically attacked, I'd have some tricks up my sleeve.

Of course, classes cost money. Talk to some studio owners if you're in a DV situation and don't have money. Tell them about your situation. Ask if you can have a discount or offer some sort of trade, like sterilizing the mats and equipment every week or producing flyers for their studio in exchange for classes. You never know until you ask, and they may need something you can offer.

Martial arts are tremendously empowering and give you great confidence. They do the same for the children. I think they're more beneficial for the children, particularly if the children are in a schoolroom setting. It not only teaches them self-defense and gives them confidence but also nullifies bullying toward them.

It's my vision that schools nationwide would adopt a curriculum that includes mandatory martial arts/self-defense training. In my mind, there's no better way to level the playing field than to have everyone trained in self defense. There will always be bullies and victims at school. But if everyone knows self-defense, a bully will think twice before he attacks someone. It would also empower abused children to know what appropriate relationships look like and how to defend themselves against inappropriate behavior.

Martial arts are tremendously empowering and give you great confidence.

Repercussions

The biggest repercussion is that the abusive and victimhood behaviors will be passed down to another generation to make yet another generation miserable. But there are a great many other possible repercussions as well: addiction to drugs or alcohol, promiscuity leading to teen pregnancy and absentee fathers, a rejection of everything you tried to teach your children as good and right, estrangement between you and your children, abandonment of religion, and so many others. These things may seem unrelated, but sadly, they're not. These things show how the mind tries to make sense of the trauma in the home, the place that's supposed to be filled with safety, love, and security—but is not. The mind bends in all sorts of ways to try to fit the two opposite things together in a way that makes sense. Inevitably, something must be rejected. Sometimes, it's what was good in the abusive situation. You would think that a child raised with abuse would see the abuse is bad and turn away from it. But that's not what happens all the time. In many cases, the bad is embraced, and the good is rejected.

The kids may reject religion because of the age-old argument, "How can a loving God allow this to happen? Therefore, there must not be a God." It's especially painful for me as a believer when children accept this false statement. God gives each of us the ability to choose for ourselves what we will think, say, do, and believe. He does not control us. Therefore, when bad things happen at the hands of other people, we cannot blame God.

Think of it this way: A business owner or a benevolent government sets up the system to provide good jobs and pay the employees/residents. There are benefits, provisions, and access to comforts and necessities, and all runs well. If an individual in that system pours poison into the water supply, is the owner or government responsible for the deaths of innocent people? No, they aren't. They may decide to take action to prevent such a tragedy again, but it's not their fault that someone in a good and decent system chose to poison the water.

Likewise, God sets the foundation and lets us choose. If we all choose to do what's good and right, good and right things prevail, and life is pleasant. If someone chooses to do bad things, everyone around that person is negatively affected. Is that God's fault? No. It's the one who chooses to do the bad things. God does not control our choices. We do.

Suppose the pain and cognitive dissonance becomes too much for the mind to handle. In that case, it will open the door to addictions, which the mind uses to numb itself from emotional, physical, and psychological pain. There's no such thing as a harmless addiction. Even activities that are not inherently bad, like shopping or working, when they become an addiction, they cause negative consequences to all who surround the individual. Addictions often lead to crime because the money it takes to support the addiction becomes less and less available, and the money must come from somewhere if the addiction is to be maintained. Thus, the stage is set for theft, prostitution, embezzlement, etc., in an ever-escalating cycle.

> *The children can be especially torn in domestic violence cases where emotional abuse is present.*

The children can be especially torn in domestic violence cases where emotional abuse is present. In my case, all my children ever wanted was their father's love. Therefore, it was withheld most of the time. He only showed kindness and affection to keep the children desperate for more. So, when I tried to divorce him, a couple of different things happened: 1) My children thought I was trying to take away any hope they had of ever having the love they craved from their father. They resented me when all I wanted to do was protect them from more cruelty. And 2) he became the dad they'd always wanted, thus reinforcing the belief that I was the bad guy, taking the one thing from them that they wanted above all else. Number one resulted from the emotional abuse they'd endured up until that point. Number two resulted from the manipulation and abuse after I tried to divorce. This was such a difficult time.

The best example of this was when my husband got an iPad and let the children watch videos with him. Most of the time, they played games like solitaire or watched a religious teacher do a talk. But now they watched videos, and it was with Dad and on his iPad. *This* was the life. My husband had moved a mattress into the dining room and was sleeping there. Our children, especially the three youngest, lay down in bed with me nearly every night for a half hour or so until I told them to go to bed. Soon, my youngest started lying down with his dad so he could watch videos. This was especially upsetting to me because I had walked in on what I suspected was a sexual abuse episode; at which time I began thinking their dad was not just mean to them but also molesting them. So, I went down, picked up my son, and brought him upstairs. My husband protested, but I was not having it.

At the time, my husband was still attending our home church, and I had stopped going because I realized the elders and teachers were supporting the abuse, not me or the children. He would take the kids with him because the kids at church were the only other children they knew. I realized I had to fight fire with fire. Wednesday was church night, so I created a tradition that I would rent or buy a movie on Wednesday nights, and we'd make popcorn and watch the movie. Dad pretty much forbade movies. If the children wanted to go to the church service, I didn't stop them, but we were going to have popcorn and movies. It didn't take long for all the children to stay home. Their dad thought that dragons and the like were demonic and sinful, so the very first video we ever watched on Wednesday night movie night was *How to Train Your Dragon*. It was awesome.

From Their Point of View

Rejecting all the good and just things you tried to teach is one of the ways children try to make sense of the situation. If the abuser says they love them and they're the parent—but they're an abuser, and they didn't act out of love—then everything they said and did was a lie. This naturally means that *everything* and *anything* could be and probably is a lie. So, children reject everything good because there's no way to tell what is the truth and what is a lie *because it all comes out of the same mouth.*

As victims, we play a role in this. Until we decide that we are, indeed, experiencing abuse and decide to take a stand against it, we're supporting the abuser in front of the children. Even when we're crying, suffering, confused, and abused ourselves, we demonstrate that the appropriate response is to accept it, stay in it, believe the abuser will get better, make excuses for the abuser, try to soften the effects of the abuse, try to protect the children as much as we can, and continue to love the abuser and communicate to the children that the abuser is a good person. We encourage the children to accept it, hope for the best, believe what the abuser says, etc. This adds to the confusion in the children's minds. They see the victim's suffering, and instead of the victim setting healthy boundaries and enforcing them, instead of the victim protecting the children from what is harmful, the victim encourages the children to lie to themselves and to convince them that it's not that bad.

But *it is* that bad! It's horrible, wrong, hurtful, mean, terrible, and any other adjective you can think of. Still, we communicate that it's not that bad, that the abuser loves us all, that love is horrible and hurtful and hateful, and that hateful, hurtful, and horrible behavior and words are good. No wonder our kids reject it all. The Bible is completely accurate when it says, "Woe to those who call evil good and good evil, who put darkness for light and light for darkness, who put bitter for sweet and sweet for bitter" (Isaiah 5:20). When we choose to remain victims, that's exactly what we're doing. And our children suffer for it.

> *Until we decide that we are, indeed, experiencing abuse and decide to take a stand against it, we're supporting the abuser in front of the children.*

This is an incredibly bitter pill to swallow. As the victim, I participated in the harm done to my children because of how I responded to the abuse. Because I chose to do what I believed to be the good and right thing to do. Because I didn't understand what the Bible says about domestic violence. I cannot express enough how important it is to understand what the Bible says about domestic violence—not what it says about interpersonal relationships in general, not what it says about Christian marriage relationships, but what it says *about domestic violence.*

Their Future

The children's future is, of course, a complete unknown. There have been good and right things that happened in their lives, along with bad and wrong things. How their minds make sense of everything is as individual as they are. But there are things you can do to help them.

First, you can separate yourself from the abusive relationship. Separating yourself and the children from the abusive situation, however you can do that, will begin the process of healing—whether it's divorce, legal separation, working with a mediator, moving out, or just gaining knowledge and starting to stand up and identify abusive behaviors and confront them as best you can. Making a break from how you've handled the situation so far is important.

Second, knowledge is power. Teach the children what you're learning. Teach them how to identify abusive behaviors and what healthy responses are to these behaviors. A child cannot tell a physically abusive parent what to do. That would be viewed as a punishable offense, and the child's life could be in danger. But let's say you start talking about physical abuse to your children: what it is, all the different ways someone can be physically abusive, and how it isn't good for anybody. Let's say your child says the abuser hurts him with a stick on the back of the legs, and that's why he always wears pants. So, you look, and sure enough, you see lines of bruises on the backs of his legs. Now you can make a plan. You can talk to the school counselors about the issue and get your child counseling. You can contact domestic violence shelters to see if they have a counselor who can help you get started on an exit plan. You can take your child to the pediatrician and show them what your child showed you. You can talk with an attorney about child abuse laws. The more evidence you have, the better your case. You can tell your child that any time it happens, they must tell you as soon as you are alone together, so you can take pictures and document it.

Teach them how to identify abusive behaviors and what healthy responses are to these behaviors.

The more your children learn and understand what's happening, the better able they are to process it healthily. It's important to identify issues and learn what appropriate behaviors are and how to protect themselves in a way that won't further endanger them. Brainstorm with them about actions you can take, and encourage them to share what they're experiencing without fear of retribution. Together, make safety plans to ensure the risk of vengeance is minimized. The children must begin the journey of awakening to reality and healing along with you. So, teach them what you are learning, learn from them, and all of you can move forward together.

A note about pediatricians, physicians, counselors, teachers, etc.: They're required to report abuse. So, if you tell a pediatrician, teacher, etc. that your spouse injured your child, your pediatrician will have to report that to Child and Family Services. I encourage developing strong relationships with these people for if and when the time comes. But I also encourage you to have a strategy here as well. You don't want your children to be put in foster care; you want your children to be safe from your abuser. So, the timing of your disclosure needs to be considered and planned and used to the best effect. At the same time, if your abuser beats up your child, you *must* disclose that, too. Be wise.

I remember my pediatrician was late to the office once because he was an expert witness in a child abuse case. The abusive parent insisted that the child's broken bones happened in an incident that didn't involve them. But our pediatrician knew that the type of broken bone couldn't possibly have resulted from the incident the abusive parent related. It could only have happened with a deliberate and violent twisting motion, which the parent's story didn't include.

Another time when I was in a therapy session, my counselor told me that what I said was something she was required to report. Did I want that? I told her no. My husband was no longer in the home, and the children were healthy and happy. To involve the courts and Child Protective Services at that point, I felt, would have been disruptive to their healing and would re-open traumatic wounds. But if my husband ever wanted to come back home, yes, I would want to report it in a heartbeat.

Each child's road to recovery will be individual and will most likely be very different from your own. In some ways, it will be like grieving after a death. After all, much dies when the truth about abusive behaviors is realized. There will be anger and denial. There will be sadness over what's lost and what could have been. There will be confusion about why it happened and why the abuser won't stop. They will think it's their fault, that they deserve it, that they brought it on, and that they do not deserve to be treated kindly or affectionately. They may blame other siblings or you for the problems and defend the abuser. They may feel a strong allegiance to the abuser, as in Stockholm Syndrome. They may be very frightened over the revelations and discussions of the truth, and they may clam up and let no one in. They may die a little inside and become very depressed. These and so many other emotions and feelings are valid and to be expected. Each child must be allowed to explore their feelings and come to terms with what's happened in their own way and time.

They must be allowed this freedom *as long as they don't become abusive in the process.* For example, they may become very angry with you and tell you you're the liar and the abuser is innocent. They can express their opinions but not yell at you, push you around, or make threats. They need to accept your opinions and the opinions of their siblings as you do theirs. They need to be willing to listen as much as they want to speak. Ground rules need to be set, so all can explore and freely express feelings, thoughts, and emotions in a way that's healthy and good for understanding and learning.

The best thing is for them to have as little contact with the abuser as possible—or no contact if possible. I strongly encourage that all communication is in writing with a third-party witness on every communication. That means texts, emails, etc.—everything in writing. No phone calls, no face-to-face conversations. And document absolutely everything.

How Your Behavior Affects the Children

I'm sure all victims have their ways of responding to the abuses they're subjected to. We each have different varieties at different levels of intensity. One thing we cannot do is turn against each other and try to compete about how badly each of us has suffered. We each have our story, and we each have our ways. While we suffered physical abuse, that was not the primary way our abuser chose to abuse us. We also experienced verbal, emotional, sexual, financial, and spiritual abuse. It's becoming more and more common to experience technological abuse. Abusers will remotely turn the heat down to 45 degrees or hack into phones, email, or social media accounts.

Before I knew better, my modus operandi was to lay low and try not to trigger anything, try not to upset him, and do what I knew he wanted as best as I could. I would placate, soothe, and smooth over anything the children did that upset him. I wouldn't look him in the eye or do anything he might think was challenging his authority. But if he started in on the children, I would usually do something to turn his ire onto me instead.

I remember sitting at the dinner table, looking down, and if I was afraid the conversation would turn harsh against the children, I looked at the one in question under my lashes. They looked at me, and we would be quiet. I remember him saying hurtful things, and we would all be quiet so he'd feel respected. What I was doing allowed the abuse to escalate. I didn't confront it. I didn't put it on his shoulders. I was not overtly and openly protecting the children. Instead, I encouraged their silence and deflected the abuse meant for them onto me. But I didn't intervene or physically and verbally stop the abuse toward them.

How you respond to the abuse is being absorbed by your children as much as the abuse is.

In my defense, I didn't know what I was dealing with, and I was trying to do what I was told the Bible said about how to relate to my spouse. Since I didn't know I was living with domestic violence, and I didn't know the Bible has specific things to say about domestic violence, I didn't know how to deal with it effectively. I wrote this book so you don't have to be in that situation.

How you respond to the abuse is being absorbed by your children as much as the abuse is. Your reactions and behavior patterns are being passed down, too, and you must be sure to respond in a way that promotes Godly, responsible, healthy behaviors instead of passive, victimhood, "everybody can feel free to trample all over me" behaviors. Take an honest and brutal look at how you respond to the abuse. Do you drop your eyes, shut your mouth, and let it happen? Do you start screaming, swearing, scratching, and clawing? Neither is good. What you want is a calm, rational, clear, emotionless statement that what just happened is abusive and to state that you won't be party to this kind of behavior anymore. You must have a safety plan in place before you do such a thing, especially if your abusive partner is particularly violent. That kind of talk can land you in the ER, so be careful and strategize. Make a plan.

Their Behavior Toward You

I love my children with everything in me. And I know they love me. They would make drawings, hug and snuggle with me at night, and want me to read to them or do this or that together. I have so many wonderful memories of me and my children when they were younger. We were mostly happy and relaxed, and we did what needed to get done with chores, school, projects, eating, cleaning, and so forth. But when Dad came home, everything changed. It was like a heavy cloud settled on the house. We were never sure what was going to happen.

The children watched and absorbed what was happening between their dad and me, which began affecting how they responded to me. Especially as they got older, they started to be dishonest with me and deliberately chose to be disobedient. For example, I once asked three of my oldest children to do a project outside. After a significant amount of time had passed and they hadn't returned, I went out to see how the project was coming. I fully expected that it would be finished or close to it.

Instead, they were outside talking, and they'd been talking the entire time. I was so mad I could have spit nails. I felt like they were treating me just like their dad did—deliberately deceiving, deliberately disobeying, and not caring that what they were doing was wrong. When I asked if they would treat other adults this way, they said no and were mad at me for calling them out. They treated me as a doormat, just like their dad did. This is another reason to act sooner rather than later. The older the children are, the more they will pick up and internalize.

Fortunately, throughout learning about domestic violence and learning to confront and oppose it, my older children began to recognize abusive behaviors for what they were. My second oldest obtained a bachelor's degree in social work, and her studies opened her eyes to the truth of what I was learning, confronting, and opposing. It's been a difficult road, but my older children have been working hard to overcome the effects of DV in their lives, and we've grown together, healed together, worked together, and, for the most part, are on fairly solid footing together. I'm so proud of the work each of my children has done to overcome what we all experienced.

Their Behavior Toward the Abuser

My children desperately longed for the safe, loving relationship they saw other kids enjoy with their dads. They just wanted to be loved. On the other hand, he was someone to be feared, not just because he hurt them so much but also because they never knew when he would hurt them and when he wouldn't. It was so unpredictable. He was distant, aloof, and much more interested in being away or being on the computer or sleeping than he was interested in any of them. Any time he was nice, acted interested in them, or got involved in something they were doing, they lapped it up like starving puppies.

But he picked favorites and targeted scapegoats. He went out of his way to reject the scapegoats as cruelly as possible. How was a mom, a submissive wife, a victim of domestic violence herself supposed to comfort a child in this predicament? They wanted so much love and positive attention, and they always opened themselves up, hoping he would respond. Then they were crushed when he said something cruel or brushed them off or turned on them.

He always told my girls how important it was to be modest because "men would undress them in their minds and lust after them." But after a time, they began to feel that *he* was the one lusting after them. It was sickening. There were so many conflicting emotions and feelings. So much they wanted, so much they feared, so much they recoiled from, so much they were creeped out by, so much hurt. Now, my boys are terrified they'll grow up to be like him, and my girls are afraid all men are exactly like that.

Are You an Accomplice?

You must cut off your feelings cold turkey and protect the children and yourself from further abuse and harm. Otherwise, you're an accomplice. You can do this, and you must. If you don't, you're just as guilty as the abuser. I understand that's a harsh reality, but it's a reality.

In psychology, there is something called the hierarchy of needs. The basic premise is that we must all have very basic life-sustaining foundational needs met before we can go on to other activities that go beyond survival. We must all know we are loved and secure before we can develop character, concentrate on getting good grades in school, or become successful in a chosen field. We, as survivors, must prioritize loving our children, providing safety and security, and providing the basic, life-sustaining necessities like food, clothing, and shelter before we can expect the children to psychologically, emotionally, mentally, and physically be able to cope with the trauma the abuse has wreaked on the child's mind, heart, and soul. We must understand that loving our children is not letting them do whatever they want. Love is not allowing them to develop bad habits or treat others poorly or be jerks. Love is not feeling sorry for them, making excuses for them, or protecting them from the consequences of their wrong choices.

The children have suffered much under the abuser's rule. It's natural to compensate for that by not requiring much from them. But regardless of what has already happened, we must still be good parents. We must still care for our children, provide for their needs, work on developing their character, praise good things and discipline not-so-good things. We must encourage them to do right and discourage them from doing wrong. We must teach them to guard their hearts but not harden them and to see and discern and understand, and not be deceived, misled, or confused by lies, half-truths, or missing information.

We don't want the cycle to repeat. We don't want our children to become victims or abusers themselves.

We don't want the cycle to repeat. We don't want our children to become victims or abusers themselves. We want them to have strong, healthy, happy relationships, and we want them to recognize toxic relationships and leave them behind. We are not only trying to learn and understand and heal ourselves but also doing the same for the children. It's a Herculean task. And many times, we need help.

Individual Abuse Toward the Children

Unfortunately, there may be abuses you don't see and the children won't talk about. It happens, and you can't go back and change it. You can't erase what has already happened. But you can change things going forward. As you and the children emerge from victimhood, you'll learn things that will make you sob, cringe, and bitterly angry. You will weep for the pain your children suffered without your knowledge. You'll feel terribly guilty for not knowing what was happening to them. You'll feel guilty for not knowing how you missed signs or that you excused odd things away, or believed the best when you should not have. You cannot help what you didn't know. You cannot change what has already happened. But you sure as heck can change things going forward.

One of the more irritating and non-sensical controlling things I learned was that my husband had told various children that they could use no more than four squares of toilet paper when they went to the bathroom. Four squares? I didn't know this until after he moved out. Naturally, I told the children they could use however much they needed to clean their potty area. But why did he do that?

Do your best to always be present whenever they have any contact with their abuser. If things seem to be going sideways, confront it immediately and get the children to a safe place away from the abuser. My children all liked to climb into bed with me to sleep. I welcomed it. For a year or so before my husband moved out, he stayed in a room in the basement while the children and I slept in the bedrooms upstairs. My youngest child was afraid to go to sleep without me in the room. Again, about two weeks after my husband moved out, my youngest started going to bed without me by himself. Curious, I asked him about it. Was he now unafraid? What was going on?

He responded, "Yeah. I'm not afraid anymore. I'm just happy. Yeah. Not afraid, just happy."

It made me cry. To think that all that time he was afraid and unhappy, and all it took was my husband being absent for two weeks, and he was no longer afraid. Things like that, and there were many, communicated to me the great impact the abuse had on my children, and I didn't even realize it until he was gone, and it stopped.

Knowledge is power. The knowledge you're gaining is your power to overcome and even thrive. You can do this. You alone will have to find the way because you alone know your circumstances and your abuser. All the options in front of you will be very hard. You will have no choice but to pick one, whether to remain as you are, go to court, fight from within, or whatever. You will choose something. And you alone will be the one who succeeds. You can do this. You can overcome. You can thrive. You can become what you were meant to become. This is a steppingstone to achieving all that you were meant to achieve.

Having children is one of the most wonderful treasures in life. And the responsibility to raise them is overwhelming, even in the best circumstances. You're dealing with much trauma. Overcoming that for yourself will be a challenge. Helping your children overcome it and keeping them safe will sometimes seem almost impossible. But you can. And you will. You will learn together, grow together, and overcome together. It will be difficult. It will be heartbreaking. It will be strengthening. It will be a wondrous adventure. It will be freeing and life-giving for all of you. It will be worth it. It *is* worth it.

15

Going Forward in Empowerment

Right now, let's pretend your abusive partner doesn't exist. You've emotionally, mentally, and physically distanced yourself, and now, you can focus on moving yourself and your children forward. Who were you before? Who are you now? Do you even know? Do you remember? You got into this relationship, and naturally, one day at a time, you changed into the person you are now without realizing a change was occurring. You'll need to make conscious decisions and conscious choices to move forward. You'll need to, very deliberately, take one step at a time to move away from toxicity and abuse toward life, freedom, and joy.

Understanding Healthy Relationships

My first piece of advice is this: Don't get into another relationship right away. You need time apart to get yourself together, figure out who you are, and get the family settled into a new routine. You need time to recover and begin the work of healing, as do your children. You need time to learn what a healthy relationship looks like and make sure you know how to behave in a healthy relationship. I'm not divorced yet, and the whole thought of being in another relationship is too scary for me to even begin thinking about, so obviously, I'm not ready for one. But some readers may feel like they need another relationship. Don't do it before you truly understand what a good relationship should be like and you're confident you won't set the stage for another abusive relationship.

My first piece of advice is this: don't get into another relationship right away.

Read, read, read. Study, study, study. Learn about yourself and what you need to change to keep yourself safe. The more you learn, the better the chances you won't fall for another predator.

Red Flags, Odd Things, and Listening to Your Gut

I met my husband when he came to my studio to repair a high-tech scanner. He was on site for several days fixing the thing, and he and the studio staff would go out after the studio closed. It was a lot of fun. When he asked me out for our first date, he requested that I wear a particular dress. I didn't see anything wrong with the request and planned to wear it.

I told my friend Pam what he said, and she said, "No way! He's trying to control you. Don't wear that dress. If I was you, I wouldn't even go out with him!" She told me, "Just watch; he's going to make a big deal of it. No way. I'd drop him like a hot potato."

Pam was right. He was trying to control me. And when I didn't wear the dress, she was right again; he made a big deal out of it. My friend had far more wisdom than I did. If you think you see a red flag, you probably do. If others see a red flag, your best bet is to listen, no matter what your heart says.

As we dated, we learned about each other. I told him that I loved dogs—shelties and collies—and after we got married, I wanted one.

He said, "I love shelties. They're so cute! We can get one right away."

When we got engaged and set a date, I asked when we could get the sheltie. He was blown away. He had no idea what I was talking about. He didn't know what a sheltie was. And he certainly was not about to get a dog. If we got any animal at all, it would be a cat. Asking for a dog upset him because his ex-wife wanted a poodle, and he got her one, and she loved the dog more than she loved him. I had no idea this would be a major pattern in my life for the next twenty-five years. If this sounds familiar, and you aren't married yet, break it off right now and don't look back.

> *If you think you see a red flag, you probably do. If others see a red flag, your best bet is to listen, no matter what your heart says.*

Trust your intuition. If something doesn't feel right, there's probably something wrong. Don't go with it. Don't be persuaded, and don't be tricked or conned. Don't go against your judgment don't go against your gut instincts. Just say, "No, that doesn't feel right to me." If he respects you, he'll let it go. If he keeps pushing, he doesn't respect you, and you need to let him go. If he doesn't respect you now, it will only get worse when you're married.

Personal Responsibility

Take responsibility for your actions. Be deliberate and intentional about your actions, and accept the consequences of those decisions and actions. You want your decisions and actions to result in good consequences, but when they don't, acknowledge the error, change it up, and do better next time.

So how does this apply right now? Whatever decisions you made that resulted in being in a domestic violence relationship probably weren't the best. To take personal responsibility, you need to make decisions and do things that will change the situation for the better. Learn what you need to change about yourself and change them. Learn what you need to identify in relationships and identify them. If getting into another relationship right now is a bad idea, acknowledge that, and don't do it. If you have things you need to do to get your children settled and your life supported apart from the abusive relationship, focus on getting those things in order. Maybe you've been a victim, but that doesn't mean you need to stay there. You can move past that and be an overcomer, but you must put in the time and effort, make the changes, and do the right things.

Personal Hierarchy of Needs

Abraham Maslow stated that physiological and safety needs must come first, which makes sense. You cannot philosophize about climate change or fossil fuels when you haven't eaten for three days, have no place to live, and it's twenty degrees outside. Physical needs must be met first regarding food, clothing, water, warmth, and the ability to sleep. Then your safety and security needs must be met. You can't get too far in entrepreneurship or pursue further education if you constantly feel in danger. Then comes belonging and relationships. You and your children must purposefully and intentionally focus on this. Your feelings of love and relationship have been grossly distorted, and you must all start over and learn what good and healthy relationships are. When you have a decent grasp on these things and work on them with purpose, new needs will arise: the need to feel you're worthy, that you've accomplished a good thing, and that you have a purpose.

Escaping domestic violence and overcoming it has done remarkable things for me. Realizing that we are so much happier and healthier without him gives me a sense of purpose and accomplishment. I recognized what was happening. I rebelled against the abuse. I persevered through everyone telling me to submit to him again. God provided a mediator and a handyman helper, and our sensei, but I was the one who accepted that help and worked to make those relationships productive for my children and me. I have a purpose larger than that now in that I want to help other victims reach self-actualization. The place to start is to satisfy the necessities of life. Get those things taken care of, and you can move on to interpersonal relationships, self-worth, and self-actualization.

Make Goals for the Future

At first, all I could do was try to get through one day at a time. The house was a wreck. Hardly any homeschooling got done. It was all we could do to survive. We poured ourselves into our new life on our farm and worked off our stresses. There were a lot of tears, conflict, fear, and uncertainty. I tried to keep a regular schedule, tried to keep us involved in martial arts, and tried to get some school in every week. Slowly, slowly, things got better.

After two years of utter chaos, we all decided we were ready to catch up on school. We were in a much better emotional place, a much better psychological place, and a much safer place. So, we set aggressive school goals and achieved them. We made decisions about the direction of the farm and started working on those goals. Instead of the farm dictating our work, our work began dictating the direction of the farm. Instead of life swinging us around by our hair, we were on our feet and decided where we wanted to go. We had come through the worst of times and done it together. We had bottomed out and were headed back up. We were going to be OK. We were going to make it.

But here's the thing: You cannot reach your goals if you don't have any. It frankly doesn't matter what your goals are. Just surviving a day is a great goal. But as you keep surviving the days, you realize you can make another goal, like having ice cream treats, or a trip to the park or McDonalds, or renting a movie, or getting something for yourself at the thrift store instead of for the kids, or having the oil changed in the car by yourself for the first time.

> *But here's the thing: you cannot reach your goals if you don't have any.*

Set some goals—small, achievable goals. Then you can build from there. For now, don't try to save the world; just do what you need to do to save yourself and your kids, one day at a time.

Family Goals

Instead of the world revolving around keeping the abuser placated, now you can set goals for your entire family. Get the children's schooling on solid ground. Help them figure out what they like and don't like and find opportunities to explore the things they like. Make chore charts or some way of dividing the labor so the household runs smoothly. Maybe have a special outing or even a short vacation. Get involved in martial arts. Brainstorm with the children to set goals for the family. Maybe you want to find an interesting job, or maybe you want to go back to school to get a degree in something you've always wanted to do. Maybe you want to subscribe to Netflix or get a new computer or a big flatscreen TV. Set goals together and gradually work toward them. You might not reach them this year, but perhaps you will next year or the year after. Keep those goals in mind, and one day, you'll achieve them, and you can look back with contentment and satisfaction and congratulate each other on how far you've come together. And safely. And without abuse or trauma.

Smash the Cycle

Unless you've made the emotional and psychological break from the relationship, there will be a tremendous pull to return to your abuser. You've invested so much. You had such high hopes and dreams, and the death of those hopes and dreams is frankly devastating. Grieving the loss is important. The relationship is dead, and it has been for a long time. The person you love never existed. You must stop trying to convince yourself that the person you love is there and will do better if you give them another chance. It doesn't work that way. He will work very hard at trying to pull you back in. He will say and do many things to suck you back in. You must be firm in your resolve and block all that out. It's another of his tricks. If he cares like he says he does, he'll let you go. Don't look back.

Don't expect yourself to be a superhero. Simply surviving might be all you can grasp for a

> *Unless you've made the emotional and psychological break from the relationship, there will be a tremendous pull to return to your abuser.*

while, and that's OK. As you learn more and gain more experience and knowledge, you'll start to climb out of the pit. One step at a time, one day at a time, one week at a time, one month at a time, and before you know it, you've been safe for a year, and things are looking up. You've got this. You really, really do. Be steadfast, unmoveable, and have the faith of a mustard seed. Rely on God, who is always, always with you, and see how He blesses you. Each day is a new day, a new chance to change and learn and grow, a new chance to love, live, bless, and be happy.

Remember *The Lion King*? In one scene, Mufasa says, "Being brave is being scared and doing it anyway." It's scary to break from what you know and step out in a new direction without your abuser. But you can learn. It can be done. You are more than capable. Before you know it, you'll learn how to live in a safe, healthy, happy, and fulfilled way apart from abuse. And you'll be so glad you did.

There will be more to untangle from than only your abusive husband. I learned that I'd also learned to accept abuse from other people. You must stop that, too. Shortly after we moved to our farm, my husband hired a neighbor with a criminal record for theft to build us a chicken coop. He shot himself in the upper thigh with a nail gun during the build. Even though he was married, he sent his wife and daughter away for a trip and asked one of my teenage daughters to come to his house and change the bandage. I happened to be talking with her when she got the text, and I said absolutely not. Absolutely no way. Over my dead body. My oldest son could go over and help him if he needed help with something, but not my teenage daughter. So, she told him no and offered the help of my oldest son. The guy promptly called my husband and told him what a b*tch I was. He'd done all this work on the coop, and when he asked for help, I wouldn't give it to him.

My husband called me, saying, "I can't believe how unkind you are being to a neighbor in distress. You need to call him back, apologize, and send (my daughter) over to his house!"

This was when I realized that I'd been groomed to accept abuse from others, and my children were also getting sucked into this behavior.

I answered, "No. I won't apologize, and I'm not sending my daughter over there. I believe he intends to rape her, and there's no way I'll put her at risk."

Happily Ever After

We all want the fairy tale. We all want love and joy and happiness from now until the day we die. That's not real life. There will be ups and downs, wonderful times, and tragedies. Times of triumph over evil and times we feel like we'll never win. But once you make the break and begin the arduous process of climbing up and out of despair, you'll also climb up and out of distress, fear, sorrow, suffering, apprehension, and trepidation. You will move forward.

You'll be brave, with little things first—like getting your first pair of new shoes in a decade—and you'll find out you can do that hard thing. So, you'll try again with something a little bigger and be able to do that, too. Your finances will start pretty rough, but things will smooth out. Finances will ease, and job situations will become better. The kiddos will have a hard time initially, but you'll all learn to handle acting out and relationship issues. You'll all begin to develop healthy ways to interact and show feelings. Relationships will strengthen, and bonds will be forged. You'll all grow, become, learn, and gain discernment and wisdom. Things will look up. And up, and up. Healing is possible, and it happens. Not only can you overcome, but you *are* overcoming!

Right now, it may not seem possible. It may be too daunting, too overwhelming, too terrifying. Just take one baby step at a time. The journey of a thousand miles begins with a single step. This isn't a sprint; it's a marathon. Put one foot in front of the other through the fear, through the evil, through everything that's coming. Just keep going!

One final word. Be thankful. Despite all the terrible things, the fear, the unknown, the sadness, etc., etc., there is *always* something to be grateful for. God inhabits the praises of His people. Sing a new song. Love life. Love your children. Love all the good things. Thank your children. Thank your friends. Thank God. Being grateful sets the tone for your journey. Sing, praise, worship, be grateful, and be watching for every beautiful, golden nugget. They will come. And you will grow, change, and become everything you were destined for.

Resources

The resources available will vary widely by where you live. The following suggestions may or may not be available in your area. Furthermore, this list is limited to resources in the United States.

If you live in a rural area, your best option will be in the nearest big city. Rural counties have very limited resources, and those they have may be overwhelmed rapidly. Resources are strained everywhere, so you must devote time to researching, calling, and emailing to find what you need and obtain it.

Ask. Ask. Ask. Ask. It never hurts to ask; the worst anybody can say is no. Keep a list of all the calls you make, what is available through whom, and what is not available and through whom. If you're only eligible for services if your family income is less than your annual household income currently, come back to that service after you're legally separated or divorced and try again.

The Internet

The internet is a huge banquet of information. Search on the following terms: domestic violence, intimate partner violence, domestic violence statistics, domestic violence in the church, and domestic violence statistics by race/gender. Use the Department of Justice criminal statistics to look up the demographics of DV abusers. There is so much information, which is so widely available, and if you cannot afford other books, the internet can educate you on virtually anything. Use it. If you cannot use it at home, most public libraries have computers with internet access available.

Here are a few websites that were particularly helpful to me:

- A spiritually directed website for victims of domestic abuse: patrickweaver.org/.
- For Christians whose marriages end due to sexual immorality or physical or emotional abuse: lifesaving-divorce.com.
- Abuse and trauma recovery coaching and courses for women in the faith community from Sarah McDugal and Bren Wise: wildernesstowild.com.

Federal Resources

- **The National Domestic Violence Hotline** (800-799-7233). It's available 24/7 with translators. Or text START to 88788. They have a website and chat available as well. The hotline is just that. They do not have a shelter or long-term housing, but they do have access to information that is local to you.
- **The National Resource Center on Domestic Violence** (800-537-2238). You can go to their websites at www.nrcdv.org and www.vawnet.org.
- **The National Indigenous Women's Resource Center** (1-855-NIWRC-99 or 406-477-3896).
- **The National Clearinghouse for the Defense of Battered Women** (1-800-903-0111, ext .3) or www.ncdbw.org. This organization specializes in helping battered women who have been charged with crimes.

They offer technical assistance, resources, and support to women and their defense teams.

There are many other national organizations. The problem with many of them is that their focus is not on individual survivors but on equipping professionals to assist survivors, which leaves you with nothing. However, sometimes they have new information. Sometimes, they can point you to a state or local resource you have not yet discovered.

State Resources

The US Department of Health and Human Services has a website that can direct you to resources in your state. Visit https://www.womenshealth.gov/relationships-and-safety/get-help/state-resources for a comprehensive list.

If you don't find your state on this list, please contact the National Domestic Violence Hotline to find a program in your area. Their phone number is 800-799-SAFE (7233).

Missouri Resources

The State of Missouri, and I'm sure most, if not all, states have lists of resources available at the local level. Check out this website for completely up-to-date information: https://dss.mo.gov/fsd/pdf/missouri-resource-guide-3steps.pdf. If you aren't a Missouri resident, you must look up your state to find what's available.

Food Assistance

If you're struggling to pay for food, help is available through the following programs:

- Food Stamp (SNAP) Benefits—A monthly benefit to help low-income households buy food. To get help through SNAP, you must apply and complete an interview. https://mydss.mo.gov/food-assistance
- Special Supplemental Nutrition Program for Women, Infants, and Children (WIC)—Provides supplemental food, nutrition education, breastfeeding promotion and support, and healthcare referrals to income-eligible women, infants, and children up to their fifth birthday. Help is available to mothers and other caregivers at wic.mo.gov.
- Food Pantries—Over 1,000 food pantries across the state provide food to those in need. You can find them at feedingmissouri.org.
- Temporary Assistance Program—Provides cash benefits to low-income families for the household's children, such as clothing, utilities, and other needs—mydss.mo.gov/temporary-assistance.
- Free and Reduced School Meals—Parents and guardians of school-aged children should complete an application to receive free or reduced-price meals at school. Sign up at the student's school for children enrolled in participating Head Start, Pre-K, and K-12 school districts.

Shelter

If you're worried about finding or keeping safe, stable, and affordable housing, these resources may help:

- If you're struggling to pay your monthly rent, HUD may be able to help—hud.gov/states/missouri/renting or call 800-955-2232.

- Shelters in Missouri can provide temporary housing while helping you find homes or apartments—homelessshelterdirectory.org/missouri.html.
- Landlord and tenant laws can help you understand your rights for repairs, evictions, deposits, etc.—ago.mo.gov/civil-division/consumer/landlord-tenant-law.

Safety

Below are resources to help make sure you and your family are safe:

- Report Child Abuse & Neglect—Anyone may report suspected child abuse, neglect, or exploitation to the Missouri Child Abuse and Neglect Hotline at 800-392-3738. This hotline is answered 24 hours a day, 7 days a week. Everyone's help is needed to keep kids safe, so if you see something, say something.
- Physical or Mental Abuse—If you or someone you know needs help with physical or mental abuse, call the National Domestic Violence Hotline at 800-799-7233.
- Sexual Abuse—If you or someone you know needs help with sexual abuse, call the National Sexual Assault Hotline at 800-656-4673.
- Suicide—if you're having suicidal thoughts or thoughts of harming yourself or others, call the Suicide and Crisis Hotline simply by dialing 9-8-8. It's available 24x7, and operators speak English and Spanish.
- Report Senior or Disabled Adult Abuse—Anyone who suspects a senior or disabled adult is being abused, neglected, bullied, or exploited should call the Missouri Department of Health and Senior Services Adult Abuse and Neglect Hotline at 800-392-0210 or report online 24/7 at health.mo.gov/abuse.

- Crime Victim Protection—The Safe at Home program helps protect crime victims by giving them a substitute address and mail-forwarding—sos.mo.gov/business/SafeAtHome/HowToApply or call 866-509-1409.
- Poison Control—The Missouri Poison Control Center helps people exposed to dangerous chemicals, drugs, and other substances find the right care as soon as possible. For emergencies, always call 9-1-1. For non-emergencies, call 800-222-1222.
- General Health—The Centers for Disease Control and Prevention has information on diseases and conditions, healthy living, traveler's health, emergency preparedness, and more—cdc.gov or call 800-232-4636.

Child Care

The following resources may help you find affordable, quality childcare:

- The Child Care Subsidy program helps with the cost of childcare so parents can focus on finding and holding steady work that can support their family's needs—https://mydss.mo.gov/qualify.
- The State of Missouri offers a one-stop website to help you do things like find a childcare facility, learn about early education programs, etc.—mo.gov/education/pre-k-and-child-care.
- United4Children provides guidance and support to families looking for childcare across the state and resources for individuals interested in opening a childcare business.—united4children.org or call 314-531-1412.
- The ParentLink WarmLine at 800-552-8522 offers support, information, and resources for parents,

caregivers, and professionals. Online developmental screening tools are available to check children's development from birth to five years of age—education.missouri.edu/parentlink or call 833-KIN-4-KID (for kinship caregivers).

Health

Taking care of your and your family's health is important to ensure you can get training and go to work as scheduled.

- Low-income families, adults, children, pregnant women, disabled individuals, and seniors may be eligible for healthcare coverage through MO HealthNet, the state Medicaid program—https://dss.mo.gov/mohealthnet/index.html.
- Community Health Centers serve individuals of all ages with coverage through Medicaid, Medicare, and private insurance—mo-pca.org/find-a-health-center.
- Missouri Department of Health & Senior Services has many helpful resources, including maternal health topics, including breastfeeding, postpartum after care and depression, and safe sleep: health.mo.gov/living/families/genetics/newbornhealth.
- Immunizations: health.mo.gov/living/wellness/immunizations.
- Youth development and teen pregnancy prevention: health.mo.gov/living/families/adolescenthealth.
- TEL-LINK, a service that provides information and referrals to help Missourians find the health services they need—health.mo.gov/living/families/tellink or call 800-835-5465.

Disabilities

- The Department of Mental Health has offices throughout the state that can help with developmental disabilities for you or a loved one—dmh.mo.gov/dev-disabilities/regional-offices or call 800-364-9687.
- You can apply for disability benefits through the Social Security Administration—ssa.gov/applyfordisability or call 800-772-1213 (TTY 573-522-9061).
- Twenty-two Centers for Independent Living (CILs) statewide offer independent living services to people with disabilities to increase their independence and their opportunity to participate in day-to-day life within their communities—mosilc.org/mo-centers-db or 888-667-2117.
- Special Health Care Needs provides health care support services, including service coordination for children and adults with disabilities and chronic illness—health.mo.gov/living/families/shcn or 800-451-0669.
- Disability Inclusion of Greater Kansas City offers Jobs Ability, an online job board designed to help those with disabilities build profiles, connect with businesses, improve their skills, and find job opportunities suited for them— centerfordisabilityinclusion.org.

Utility Assistance

Being unable to pay your current or past utility bills can lead to lost employment, endanger persons in your household if there are shutoffs, and impact your future.

- The Low-Income Home Energy Assistance Program (LIHEAP) may be able to help eligible Missourians

- pay their energy bill—https://mydss.mo.gov/utility-assistance.
- The Missouri Public Service Commission offers energy efficiency and assistance programs—psc.mo.gov/General/Energy_Efficiency_Assistance_Programs or call 800-392-4211 (TTY 573-522-9061).
- The Affordable Connectivity Program (ACP) helps low-income households pay up to $30 a month—https://www.fcc.gov/acp.

Mental Health

Mental wellness is important so you can take care of your needs, succeed in your future, and work with others.

- If you or someone you know needs help, consider contacting a local Community Mental Health Center—dmh.mo.gov/mental-illness/help/community-mental-health-centers.
- The Department of Mental Health offers resources to help with suicide prevention, alcohol and drug treatment, coping with disasters, and veterans in crisis—dmh.mo.gov/crisis-assistance or call 800-364-9687.
- If you are thinking about suicide, are worried about a friend or loved one, or need support, call the National Suicide Prevention Lifeline by dialing 988 or go to dmh.mo.gov/mental-illness/suicide/prevention.

Parenting

Creating a healthy foundation for lifelong mental health and wellness for Missouri's youth is important, and many resources are available to support parents.

- Early Connections offers helpful resources for parents to ensure that Missouri's children grow up healthy and happy—both mentally and physically—earlyconnections.mo.gov.
- ParentLink has quality parenting information, materials, outreach activities, and support groups at no cost—education.missouri.edu/parentlink or call 573-882-7322.
- Child Support can help locate parents, establish paternity, enforce orders, and distribute collections—dss.mo.gov/child-support or call 800-859-7999.
- JAG-Missouri helps students reach their full potential by providing extra guidance, helping for classroom success, and providing work-based learning in many middle school, high school, and alternative school programs, resulting in increased graduation and employment rates—jag-missouri.org or call 417-425-5139.
- Alternatives to Abortion helps women carry their unborn child to term and assists them with caring for their child or placing their child for adoption if they choose. Services are available during pregnancy and for one year following birth. Services include help with childcare, domestic abuse protection, education services, paternity, food housing and utilities, transportation, and parenting skills—dss.mo.gov/fsd/a2a.
- Some communities have crisis care facilities, which is a free service to families and is designed to ease immediate crisis or emergencies. Crisis care can also help the family prevent future crises or emergencies—dss.mo.gov/cd/keeping-kids-safe/crisis-care-for-families.htm.

Legal

Legal issues, both past and current, can impact your ability to find training or work.

- The Missouri Legal Services provides free legal help—lsmo.org or call 800-444-0514 (Eastern MO), 816-474-6750 (Western MO), 800-568-4931 (Mid-MO), or 800-444-4863 (Southern MO).

Vital Records

The Department of Health and Senior Services can provide you with a copy of your birth certificate or other records for a fee. You will need your birth certificate to get the photo ID (drivers and non-driver's license) you will need for training, employment, state benefits, doctor visits, etc—health.mo.gov/data/vitalrecords or call 573-751-6387.

Unemployment

You can file an unemployment claim online as soon as you are separated from your employer. UInteract, the online claim filing system, is mobile-friendly and available 24 hours a day—uinteract.labor.mo.gov or call 800-320-2519.

Transportation

Without reliable transportation, starting or continuing employment or training can be impossible. MO Rides can help connect you to local transportation services—morides.org/search or call 844-836-7433.

Veterans

- The Missouri Benefits & Resources Portal helps service members, veterans, and their families find benefits and local resources—veteranbenefits.mo.gov or call 573-522-4061.
- The Veterans Administration (VA) supports veterans and their loved ones through health care, housing, employment, education, and more—va.gov or call 800-698-2411.

Technology

Technology such as phones, the internet, and digital resources is essential for online learning, applying for jobs, increasing skills, and managing your household. Some resources can help you get the technology you need. Reduced or no-cost phone services may be available in your area. There are free trainings to help with things like learning about computers and software, job search, career planning, help with applying and interviewing for jobs, and more. There are many options for connecting to employers, classmates, teachers, physicians, family members, and others. The following are websites that offer video conferencing: skype.com, zoom.us.

Finances

Several organizations can help teach families how to effectively use income to meet today's needs and build their savings account.

- Missouri Bankers Association helps families create personalized financial plans—mobankers.com/MBA/

AboutMBA/MBAMembership/Young_Bankers_Division/Financial_Literacy.
- FDIC Money Smart can help you plan for savings, meet unplanned expenses, use credit wisely, apply for loans and more—fdic.gov/resources/consumers/money-smart/index.html.
- Earned Income Tax Credit (EITC) can give low- and moderate-income working families a financial boost—irs.gov/credits-deductions/individuals/earned-income-tax-credit.
- Low-income and elderly Missourians can get help preparing Missouri tax returns—dor.mo.gov/personal/tax_assistance_information.php or call 800-906-9887 or 888-227-7669.
- The Federal Trade Commission Consumer Information allows you to get your credit report for free once a year—consumer.ftc.gov.
- NFCC is a non-profit organization that may be able to help if you are struggling with excessive credit card or other debt—nfcc.org or call 800-388-2227.
- The Missouri State Treasurer's Financial Literacy Portal aims to empower Missourians with the information, skills, and habits to be financially successful—treasurer.mo.gov/financial-literacy.

Education and Career

Services are available to help you build and develop your skills no matter what stage of your career.

- To complete high school, The Department of Elementary and Secondary Education provides information on

how to prepare for and take your High School Equivalency Test (HiSET)—hse.mo.gov or call 573-751-3504.
- Career and Technical Education Services helps youth and adults gain career skills and enter the workforce—dese.mo.gov/financial-admin-services/career-and-technical-education-cte-finance or call 573-751-3500.
- Excel Centers allow adults the opportunity to earn their high school diploma. While earning their diploma, participants can also earn college credits and receive industry-recognized certifications that will increase their ability to get self-sustaining employment—excel.mersgoodwill.org or call 314-655-4820 (St. Louis), 417-862-5005 (Springfield), 573-686-6004 (Poplar Bluff), 573-499-1220 (Columbia), 573-271-5220 (Cape Girardeau), or 314-967-2005 (Florissant).
- English as a Second Language (ESL) can help you find Missouri schools and free ESL programs in Missouri—esldirectory.com/esl-program-search/usa/Missouri.
- The Department of Elementary and Secondary Education (DESE) provides information on the Adult Education and Literacy (AEL) Program, which provides free assistance to adults who need basic skills such as reading, writing, math, and English language— ael.mo.gov or call 573-751-1249.
- For help finding your career path, The Talify Skills assessment can help you learn more about your personal work skillset—jobs.mo.gov/talify or call 888-728-5627.
- Resources are available to help you identify and explore options if you are looking for a new career path. Jobs League can help teens and young adults learn about careers and get work experience—mydss.mo.gov/jobs-league-program or call 888-728-5627.

- Job Corps helps students train for technical jobs through four locations in Missouri—jobcorps.gov or call 800-733-JOBS.
- SkillUP helps Food Stamp (SNAP) recipients get free help with skills, training, and employer connections to get a job or a better job—on.mo.gov/skillup.
- The Missouri Work Assistance (MWA) helps temporary assistance recipients become ready for a job, get real work experience, find employment, and keep a job—mydss.mo.gov/missouri-work-assistance.
- Missouri Job Centers offer services to help people gain and/or improve skills needed to succeed in the workplace—jobs.mo.gov/career-centers.
- Missouri Vocational Rehabilitation specializes in employment and training services that can assist eligible individuals with disabilities achieve and maintain successful employment—dese.mo.gov/adult-learning-rehabilitation-services/vocational-rehabilitation/vocational-rehabilitation-offices or call 877-222-8963.
- Missouri Community Colleges offer employment and training programs and certificates—www.missouricolleges.org/.
- Missouri Registered Apprenticeships can help you learn important trade skills while earning a paycheck—jobs.mo.gov/content/moapprenticeships or call 866-506-0251.
- Employment and training services are available to help Missourians with developmental disabilities, mental health, or substance use disorders—dmh.mo.gov/about/employment-services or call 800-207-9329 (Developmental Disabilities) or 800-575-7480 (Behavioral Health).
- Rehabilitation Services for the Blind helps visually impaired Missourians get training, education, and

technical help to find great employment and live independently—dss.mo.gov/fsd/rsb.
- Credential Completion and Employment Financial Assistance Program is a short-term program to help youth who exited foster care earn a recognized credential or specialized training that leads to employment—dss.mo.gov/cd/older-youth-program/credential-completion-assistance.htm or call 800-950-4673.
- Missouri Connections supports the career development efforts of schools, community organizations, and adult job-seeker programs. It helps individuals learn about their talents, skills, and interests and makes the connection between planning for continued education and the work world—missouriconnections.org.
- If your employer moved your job out of the United States or eliminated your job due to foreign competition, Trade Adjustment Assistance may help—jobs.mo.gov/trade-adjustment-assistance or call 888-728-5627.
- Journey to College resources from the Missouri Department of Higher Education & Workforce Development provide information to help plan and pay for college—journeytocollege.mo.gov.

Again, these lists of resources have limitations in what they can offer you as a survivor. But take every crumb of information you can and explore it. If legal assistance is mentioned, continue digging until you find who offers what and how to access it. If food stamps are mentioned, go to the office and determine if you qualify. You will need to do the phone calling and legwork. It may be that not much is available to you. But at the very least, you can call family court attorneys for a free twenty- or thirty-minute consultation. Call your closest domestic violence shelter and meet with the advocates there to develop a strategy. If you've got some money stashed away, talk to an accountant or your bank about how to protect it. You have tools and the ability to find more information. The ball is in your court now. Get it done!

Further Reading

Following is a list of useful online articles, some of which are quoted in this book.

- **Missouri Domestic Abuse Response Team:** https://www.slmpd.org/dart.shtml
- **Documenting Abuse in Preparation for Court:** https://www.techsafety.org/preparationforcourt
- **Women Who Kill in Response to Domestic Violence: How Do Criminal Justice Systems Respond?** https://www.penalreform.org/resource/women-who-kill-in-response-to-domestic-violence/http://websites.umich.edu/~clemency/position.html
- **Marissa Alexander's story:** www.freemarissanow.org
- **Demographics and Domestic Violence:** https://www.domesticshelters.org/resources/statistics/demographics-and-domestic-violence
- **Family Violence Statistics:** https://bjs.ojp.gov/content/pub/pdf/fvs.pdf
- **1-in-4 Highly Religious U.S. Marriages Have Abuse:** https://lifesavingdivorce.com/1in4/
- **Domestic Abuse in the Church a 'Silent Epidemic':** https://www2.cbn.com/news/us/domestic-abuse-church-silent-epidemic

- **Domestic Violence Statistics:** https://www.thehotline.org/stakeholders/domestic-violence-statistics/
- **Domestic Abuse: 4 Things Pastors and Churches Need to Know:** https://www.bcne.net/news/domestic-abuse-4-things-pastors-and-churches-need-to-know

Acknowledgments

My dear friends, you have come on an incredible journey with me. The first acknowledgment I want to make is to you, the reader. Without you, your determination, grit, and courage, the world would continue as it is. But with you, the world can become a better place.

I want to acknowledge my children, who have endured so much and are also walking out the other side in their own time and way. I am so proud of them.

The three men God used so instrumentally in our lives: Scott Nolda, Steve Yager, and Rob Kee. We are changed because of you—more than you can possibly know.

Wendy Everts, who read parts of my first draft and believed in the power of the work and encouraged me to write and publish it.

Nancy Erickson, my publisher and editor, has steadfastly worked with me during my fears, delays, financial struggles, and avoidance of working through the difficult sections, and has helped me produce something so much better than what I started with.

Jennifer, my counselor extraordinaire, has seen things, addressed things, confronted things, and encouraged me, chastised me, corrected me, strengthened me, and is letting me continue to work out my healing under her expert guidance. I am so grateful.

My new friends in my new home in Silva who hired me, worked with me, let me cry and complain to them, told me wonderful things, and gave me hugs and encouragement in so many big and small ways. They showed me I can be happy again.

Greg Wilson, who quietly transformed my life without even knowing it.

David Williams enabled me to get through reliving everything during the final editing process. I was a wreck, and he kept me on track.

To all of you, I cannot fully express how you have each impacted my life and were so deeply instrumental in saving me in one way or another. I am so, so grateful for each of you.

About the Author

Above all else, Rebecca Commean is a mother and a redeemed child of God. Born in 1965, she married in 1990 and raised a family who lived the life described in this book. She has nine children, most of whom are grown and have moved away from home. She lives on a farm in Southeast Missouri, where she and the children who are still at home raise beef and dairy cattle, sheep, goats, chickens, livestock guardian dogs, and cats. Growing her farm business is her main job, but writing books is becoming an increasing passion. She enjoys being outside with her animals and plants, soaking in the beauty and peace of the Missouri countryside, and planning for the future.

Printed in the USA
CPSIA information can be obtained
at www.ICGtesting.com
LVHW010258151123
763986LV00087B/2757

9 781955 711296